Radiant Wildheart

Radiant Wildheart

A GUIDE TO AWAKEN YOUR INNER ARTIST AND LIVE YOUR CREATIVE MISSION

SHEREEN SUN

HAY HOUSE, INC.

Carlsbad, California ✦ New York City

London ✦ Sydney ✦ New Delhi

Published in the United States by: Hay House, Inc.: www.hayhouse.com®
Published in Australia by: Hay House Australia Pty. Ltd.: www.hayhouse.com.au
Published in the United Kingdom by: Hay House UK, Ltd.: www.hayhouse.co.uk
Published in India by: Hay House Publishers India: www.hayhouse.co.in

Cover design: Kathleen Lynch
Interior design: Julie Davison
Interior illustrations: Alexis Rakun and Jessie Caballero

Cataloging-in-Publication Data is on file at the Library of Congress

Tradepaper ISBN: 978-1-4019-6346-0
E-book ISBN: 978-1-4019-6347-7
Audiobook ISBN: 978-1-4019-6962-2

10 9 8 7 6 5 4 3 2 1
1st edition, March 2023

Printed in China

I dedicate this book to my magical and creative inner
child who longed to be seen, understood, and loved.
To the artist inside of each of us who deserves to feel safe
enough to be expressed. To everyone who has courageously
lived their truth, even when it meant breaking tradition
and being the first. To the dreamers, the misfits, the rebels,
and the highly sensitive ones who've spent a
lifetime searching for where they belong.

This one's for you.
I'll advocate for you forever.

Contents

Dream Foreword
by SARK

Radiant Wildheart is an awakening beacon to your sovereign creative soul. I see Shereen and her book as a vital voice showing us how to live our whole lives creatively. Shereen expands the scope of what creativity is beyond the visual arts and into a new way of living.

I invite you to wake up and take your powerful place in these pages, and in the pages of your heart. Create and share the boldness you have always dreamed of. This book will activate you.

Immerse yourself in Shereen's inspiring stories and journey, and let them awaken and accelerate yours to even more *awe*.

Listen deeply to the current that runs throughout this book. It's an invitation to be you, and to let that you be fully seen and known now.

And when being fully seen gets scary—and it will—keep going and growing. Your Radiant Wildheart will burst open again and again, and there will be no end to your experiences of transformation.

I'm so very glad that Shereen bravely moved with and through the many challenges that could have obfuscated the creation of this book. She discovered a new way of radiantly living for herself, and she describes it beautifully, and in practical ways that others can now follow.

I am honored to have mentored Shereen in parts of her creation process with this book, and to be writing this Foreword.

Within these pages, you will find an extravagant collection of directions and innovative concepts to support and inspire your most mighty creations. Shereen *lives* these directions and concepts, so they've all been tested in real life for you.

Explore the ways you are already a Sacred Rebel within and beyond your lineage, now and forever.

Take her Elemental Archetype quiz and discover your type. Mine is a blend that results in me being described as a Mystic Visionary.

Meet and understand your "Inner Overprotectors," and open your mind and spirit to reenvision what you thought was stopping you. Allow yourself to experience new ways to continue in your true power.

Feel completely your wildness and join your Divine Purpose Path toward your Creative Mission. Shereen is beautifully embodying her Creative Mission, and she shows you how to do and live more of your mission too. As she says, "The magic is in the stretch."

Let yourself see and transform your sacred creative wound as you welcome six different kinds of abundance. This book has uniquely designed Expansion Exercises to catalyze your own creative revolution.

I'm grateful for Shereen and this blessed book's insightful guidance that will help you center fun and learn more about the importance of your pleasure activation. Shereen shows you how to welcome and expand your deepest desires and to live in those ways. And as she eloquently says, "*Be* time is the new *me* time."

I also appreciate this book for the many ways it supports creating and community building. Shereen teaches a sacred weaving of "me to we" and shows you how to build and share your creative movement.

As you engage in the Spirals of Support described in this book, you will realize that you are not alone, and that you are truly a Radiant Wildheart, being liberated from within. Let Shereen's beautifully uncommon book be part of your evolving wing structure as you uplift yourself in creative flight.

Love, SARK

RADIANT

/ˈrā-dē-ənt/

adjective

Sending out light; shining or glowing brightly.

WILD

/wīld/

adjective and adverb

A natural state. Uninhibited. To grow without restraint.

HEART

/härt/

noun

The central or innermost part of something. The vital part or essence. The heart regarded as the center of a person's thoughts and emotions, especially love, compassion, or loyalty.

RADIANT WILDHEART

/ˈrā-dē-ənt/ /wīld/ /härt/

noun

An earth angel that is bold, fearless, and unapologetic in being all of themselves. Willing to take the unconventional path. An honest stand for self-expression and not afraid to be seen. Healers of their lineage with limitless potential to make an impact during their time on Earth. Born to be of service. Treat themselves with deep love and reverence, knowing that their divine offerings can change the world.

Author's Note

Welcome, Wildheart. What you hold in your hands is a quintessential guide to help you fall in love with your life and find your confidence as an artist. If you're here, you're a creative spirit on a mission to make the world better. We are all artists longing to be expressed and seen for our gifts. You might not feel creative yet, but I know you are. And I want to help you see that for yourself. No matter where you are on the journey, you are welcome here.

I define **Radiant Wildheart** as a bold and creative being who is on a brave mission to take the unconventional path toward full self-expression in service to collective liberation and personal healing, always with a deep reverence for how our gifts can change the world. As a **creativity** mentor and dream activator for over 15 years, I've had the privilege of working with thousands of Radiant Wildhearts to help them manifest their most powerful creative vision and step into a role of Artist of their Life. I do this work because I see them and I see you. I feel your deep desire for liberation on every level—creatively, spiritually, physically, and financially. I know that you want to express yourself with total confidence so you can finally stop second-guessing yourself and getting in your own way.

Bring your insecurities and self-doubt because we are about to embark on a deep healing journey to find the real you underneath any fears you might have. We are going to radically shift your mindset and beliefs so that you can become an unstoppable force for magic in the world.

Introduction

Finding the Courage to Create

YOU'RE AN ARTIST, AND YOUR LIFE IS A WORK OF ART

Even when it seems like the world has gone nuts, there is one thing that I know is true: at the core of my being, I am an artist. And I don't just mean that I can paint or draw; in fact, I've never been particularly great at representational drawing. What I mean is that I make empowered creative choices about how I want to live my life and spend my time. My life is my greatest masterpiece. But that wasn't always the case. For most of my life, I was lost, confused, and depressed. I was convinced no one understood me, and no matter how hard I tried I couldn't see a way forward . . . that is, until one magical night when I was 16 years old hanging out with my dear friend Cheez.

You see, when I was in high school, I just couldn't seem to figure things out. I was (secretly) a **queer** kid who didn't feel like there was anywhere I belonged. All I really wanted to do was make art. But I wasn't one of those talented kids. At the time I couldn't paint or sing or play an instrument. I had never really even given myself permission to try. I watched all these amazing artists around me and wished I was more like them.

It wasn't until I started connecting with other artists that I began the process of healing my relationship with my creativity. Growing up in

Las Vegas was full of bright lights, vibrant colors, and underground parties where artists hung out. Cheez was the first artist friend I ever made during a shy freshman year in my new public school. We would take the bus on adventures to local record stores or thrift shops, and then head back to her parents' house. Her parents were a very traditional immigrant family from China, but Cheez was anything but traditional. Her room was filled with paint and colorful, dripping canvases. We spent hours waxing poetic about our theories of the universe and human consciousness. And we would sneak out after her parents had gone to bed and explore the underground art scene in our city until the sun came up.

One time after a wild night out in the Las Vegas desert, Cheez and I were sitting in her room talking. I could feel a desire to create and express myself building in my body and tightening in my throat. When I finally worked up the courage to ask Cheez if she would teach me to draw, her eyes twinkled as she got up to grab a pen and giant piece of paper.

At first she started drawing a circle here and a circle there of different sizes. But as she moved across the page, the circles overlapped and started to form into something bigger and magical—a sense of connection out of the chaos, a sense of possibility. Cheez looked at me earnestly and said, "Circles equal truth." I could see that she was drawing me and all those disconnected parts of myself were waiting to be connected. At that moment, my creative self took a step forward and an artist was born.

Of all my intersecting identities, being an artist is the one that feels most like home to me. You might think that since I am a painter and a musician, I would naturally be able to tap into my creative powers. But the truth is, stepping into my **inner artist** has taken a lifetime of commitment, practice, and being willing to shed lots of tears. And I still doubt myself. I still wonder if I have anything meaningful to say or if anyone will really want to listen to me. I now know that this is a very normal part of the creative process. And that pretty much all of the artists, creatives, and culture makers that I admire go through the same thing on a regular basis.

So many of us are walking through the world with fractured creativity. The fracturing of our creativity is a gradual process that most of us experience in our childhood. As babies, we draw with wild abandon and sing as loud and emphatically as we want. We don't care if what we are creating is award worthy. We just want to express ourselves. As we get older, we get more self-conscious and self-critical. We judge ourselves and we judge one another. And we live in a world that profits off those insecurities. When the world has told you your whole life that you are small, it takes a lot of effort to remind yourself that you are a mighty soul with an important message to share.

To me, creativity is open-ended. I want to be clear that when I am talking about creativity, I am not just talking specifically about the visual arts. So many people only think of the arts as living on a canvas or in a sketchbook, but we are going to blow that definition wide open. Creativity is a way of life and a state of mind. It's a lens through which you can look at absolutely anything and everything. Your creativity is not confined to any traditional media for making art. In fact, the choices you make when you are cooking your food, parenting your kids and fur-babies, or living out your morning routine are all highly creative acts and opportunities to be a little more self-expressed.

By healing my fractured creativity and reclaiming my inner artist, I've found myself again and again. If you're here, my sense is that you are ready to come back to your wholeness and remember your inner artist again too. And I want to show you that in doing so, you have the potential to spark your own creative revolution. One that not only impacts you, but also everyone who is blessed to encounter your creations. And when you do, your whole world becomes a little more saturated with color, depth, and beauty. Because there is no better way to make your life more meaningful than to connect to something bigger than yourself.

If you're reading this book, there is likely a movement to live out loud brewing inside of you too. But maybe you don't think you are an artist. Maybe you don't believe that you have any talent (you don't need any). Maybe you think you can't create anything beautiful (beauty is subjective). Or maybe you are just afraid (of how powerful you are).

I want to show you that every moment is an opportunity. And without realizing it, you make artistic choices all the time. There are no two people in the world who put their lives together in exactly the same way. Whether you have realized it or not, you are the artist of your life and everything you do is a creative act. You are a creator, and you can make your visions a reality.

You are at the start of an incredible journey. And I am here to help you walk your divine path toward living your **Creative Mission** every day and in every way. This book will help you remember who you truly are, liberate yourself with your creative practices, and embody your Creative Mission fully. If you're someone who has always wanted to call yourself an artist or express yourself more clearly in the world, I'll help you see that you're so much more creative than you give yourself credit for. By the end, you'll be ready to paint your world in Technicolor and live your most unapologetic and expressed life, knowing that when you do, you heal yourself and create your world in alignment with your truth. And finally, you'll be ready to put all of this magic into sacred service, and help others find more freedom in their own lives too.

WELCOME TO YOUR DIVINE PURPOSE PATH

Each person's **Divine Purpose Path** looks completely different, and a lot of times, you don't (and won't!) even know exactly where you are headed. Your Divine Purpose Path is the imaginary winding and curving road that represents your unique journey toward living your Creative Mission. Along your path, you'll find all the breakthroughs, breakdowns, moments of bliss, hard lessons, and ecstatic experiences that have made you who you are. As you move forward on your path, you'll begin to meet all of the amazing beings you'll connect with and inspire through your creative liberation. Your path won't always be clear, but if you keep taking the steps forward, it will always magically appear before you.

Walking your Divine Purpose Path is going to help you figure out what makes you come alive. When you recommit to your Creative Mission and honor what you were put here on Earth to do, you will actually create the world that you want to see . . . instead of just dreaming about it! This book is the magical life map to sparking your own unique, creative spirit-led revolution. Together, we'll take this process step-by-step so that you will feel crystal clear and empowered to move forward with confidence and wild creativity.

Please know this is a space that is welcoming of all genders represented on the spectrum. The Radiant Wildheart community is full of deep feelers, activists, healers, intuitives, artists, BIPOC, queer and trans* folx, and anyone who wants to speak up for the liberation of all beings. My intention is to be inclusive with gender-neutral language, and non-binary and gender-nonconforming creatives are always welcome here. Most of the time, you might see me using the gender-neutral pronouns they/them, and there might be some occasions where I use the pronouns she/her. This is because there is a lot of divine femme energy here in Radiant Wildheart space—meaning, we approach life with intuition, creativity, and flow. However, these qualities are accessible to everyone and are nongendered. Just know, being inclusive of my queer & trans* community is a priority for me, and I hope it is for you too.

HOW TO USE THIS BOOK

This book has four sections. In Section 1, you will uncover your Creative Mission and understand what that means for your life. You will meet your elemental archetype so that you can better harness your creativity. In Section 2, you will awaken your inner artist and discover who you are and what it is that you stand for. You'll recognize the vision you have for your life and root it deeply into your own personal **ethos**. Section 3 is all about liberating yourself. This is where you will really begin to cultivate your creative practice. This is also where you will begin to get your creativity out of your heart and into the world. In Section 4, you'll start living your Creative Mission out loud, taking all of the brilliance you've been nurturing and putting it into service. This is also where you will develop your leadership skills and begin to use all of your creativity to lift others up so your sparkly, creative life can impact others and inspire them to be more liberated too. Throughout these pages, you'll also find bolded words that are defined at the end in the Glorious Glossary.

You are encouraged to make this book work *for you*. If that means reading it in a non-linear fashion by flipping through the pages and paragraphs at random, great! If that means you want to start by just exploring the artwork and chapter titles, fabulous! I acknowledge that we are all different types of learners and readers. Whatever way you engage with these concepts is perfect. And I believe that even if this book ends up sitting on your bookshelf for a month or two, it will still impact you with its magical energy.

Exercises in this book are open-ended and are for your eyes only. Nothing you create here will be graded, and you don't need to show anything to anyone unless (and until!) you feel like it. I want to encourage you to listen deeply to your own process, while also making sure to stretch! **Stretching** is doing something that's just slightly out of your comfort zone, like setting an extra-lofty goal for yourself or being brave and doing something that scares you simply because it will help you grow and evolve. Stretching is a way of life, and I want to invite you to take the stretch when the opportunity presents itself. Nothing is going to be put in front of you that you can't handle. You're *that* powerful.

> # The magic is in the stretch.

I've filled this book up with creative practices for you to try out. Most of them are short and simple but will infuse you with lots of inspiration. All of them have the potential to transform your life. To live a creative life means to practice. A common phrase said around yoga is, "The most difficult part of your yoga practice is showing up to the mat." The same is true for your creativity. The most difficult part about being an artist is showing up consistently enough to progress. But, after enough time, your creative habits will become second nature. If you fall off the wagon or skip out on a practice, let it go! Building up your creative habits takes time. For me, it's taken years. But you can always circle back to this, so release your inner Perfectionist and just commit to showing up.

Tip: One of the ways that I make my creative practice more accessible is by setting up different creative centers in my house. At any point, I can pick up an instrument or a paintbrush and make some art for five minutes. You can find me taking dance breaks to my favorite songs from my teenage years or jumping on my rainbow trampoline throughout the day to set the vibe and move my energy. When I get out of my head and into my body, new ideas and inspiration begin to flow. While it's challenging to get started and stick with it, if you keep showing up to your creative and pleasure-filled practices, confidence will find you.

Here's what you'll find within these pages to help you liberate your radiant heart and unleash your wild creative magic into the world:

Abundance Journal Prompts

I recommend finding yourself an **Abundance Journal** to accompany you on the journey of completing this book. An Abundance Journal is any kind of magical notebook that makes you feel absolutely open and free to go deeper into your creative process. My journal has gold leaf and just feels fancy. I recommend handwriting, because there is something magical and transformative about the hand in tapping into the mind-body connection. Throughout the book, there will be specific prompts for you to complete in your Abundance Journal, but you can use your journal for anything, including sketching, brainstorming, collaging, doodling, self-reflection, and whatever else your heart desires. Carry it with you as you work through the chapters to jot down all of your inspired ideas. Let your Abundance Journal be filled with the inner workings of your brilliant mind and shining heart so that you can always reflect on your growth and evolution.

Inner Overprotectors

You might be familiar with your inner critics, the many voices in your head that tell you you're not enough or not ready to take the next step into creative greatness. I like to refer to these beings as **Inner Overprotectors** (IOPs) because they don't mean to cause you harm. In fact, those parts of yourself that might feel afraid, full of self-doubt, or deep in impostor syndrome are incredibly important to your creative liberation. Their role is to protect you and help you, keeping you safe from potential harm. Once you identify who they are, you can begin to understand your IOPs and how they are trying to be of service to you. Then you can separate yourself from them and embrace as quirky friends, rather than trying to fight them.

Take a moment now and ask yourself, *What are my Inner Overprotectors trying to tell me?* Can you see them as a reminder for how loved you are, and thank them for trying to keep you safe? When you separate these thoughts from yourself, they won't hold you back anymore. You will never be fully rid of Inner Overprotectors, but you can change your relationship with them to be more nurturing and supportive for both of you.

Expansion Exercises

Each chapter of this book features an expansion exercise that will help you evolve as an artist. I believe that real transformation happens not just from doing the inner work, but also by getting your creations out into the world and being seen in your magic. The expansion exercises are meant to take your learning even further. So they feel expansive, try them on and see what emerges.

WELCOME MISTAKES AND TRUST YOUR PROCESS

One of my main principles when teaching creativity is *process over product*. I am much less interested in the finished result or how beautiful the final project looks than I am in how you felt while you were creating it. I believe every aspect of your journey is sacred and important for your remembering who you truly are. I want to invite you to cultivate a light-hearted attitude and a sense of playfulness as you witness your own process. The more fun you have, the more flow you will find in your creative journey. I encourage you to experiment, try new things, and hold it all lightly. Be curious and treat your Creative Mission like a fun research project to discover what lights you up and turns you on with aliveness and inspiration. Your confidence will develop with time, as long as you remember that the only way you can fail is if you quit or never even start.

Mistakes are an important part of the creative process. And the good news is, any and every mistake can be corrected, and almost any challenge can be resolved. Expect challenges. Embrace them. I've made huge mistakes on my journey, but I'm grateful for all of them because they made me into the resilient and badass Radiant Wildheart that I am today! These moments where you feel stretched are in service to you and your evolution. With each challenge, you'll learn something new. And yes, there may be moments where you'll want to put the proverbial paintbrush down and never pick it back up again. But you can and you will.

Every step of your journey is sacred.

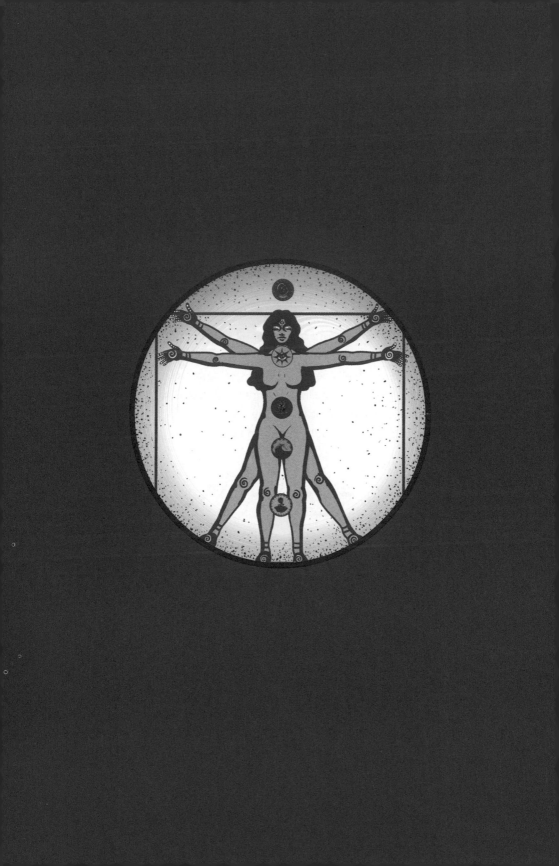

PART I

Spark Your Creative Revolution

CHAPTER ONE

We Are the Wild Ones

"In diversity, there is beauty and there is strength."

— MAYA ANGELOU

YOUR CREATIVE MISSION

Every single person on this planet arrives with a sacred Creative Mission—a reason for why you are here that was whispered into your ear before you were born. When you live in alignment with your Creative Mission, you flourish. When you live in opposition to your Creative Mission, you struggle and feel incomplete.

Your Creative Mission is where your creativity intersects with your drive to make a difference in this world. It wasn't until I found my Creative Mission that I realized that I too am an artist and that I can create something world changing. And while I love to paint and practice my guitar, my primary creative medium is my life.

I'm going to help you discover your Creative Mission. We need you to sing out and to share your message, to be unapologetically expressed and liberated to create the world you want to see. I know it can feel scary sometimes, but I will be with you every step of the way. And I know that this will be worth it for you. Here's what I can promise you will get from the book.

First, you will be able to build a life that fits your Creative Mission. We all know what it feels like to be out of alignment with what you're truly here to do. This book will help you affirm what is uniquely yours to do and create it. Really! You can take that idea and make it real. And while it will take some work from you, it's closer than you think.

Second, you will be able to have a bigger impact in the world. Now, I know this might sound intimidating. Maybe your world is your family, your community, or your town. Or maybe you've got a message that you want to spread globally. No matter the size of your dream, when you are living your Creative Mission, you can touch more people more deeply. And that's really what it's all about, isn't it—making a difference? Otherwise, what's the point?

Third, you'll learn how to express yourself so that your radiant heart shines through. You'll be able to share your message with more clarity, authority, and relevance. I know you have something powerful to say. That's part of having a Creative Mission in the world. I can show you how to embrace what you want to share and get your authentic message to people in a way that's fun and engaging, and inspires you to keep showing up for what you believe in.

Fourth, you'll become more confident. Can you imagine standing on a stage in front of a thousand people telling them a story from your life? For most of us, this idea is terrifying. But sharing your story is one of the most powerful ways for people to connect to you and your work. I'll teach you how to let your Creative Mission fuel your desire to speak up, helping to turn your fear into excitement. And don't worry, you never have to speak in front of a thousand people, but you'll be ready if you want to.

And **finally**, you'll feel more like yourself in every aspect of your life. Most people I meet have been hiding from their Creative Mission for a good part of their lives. But that's like putting part of yourself in a box and not letting anyone see it . . . including yourself. When you let yourself show up fully, wild and expressed, you feel more alive, more authentic, and more like *you*! That's the place where all the magic begins.

I want you to see yourself as a Radiant Wildheart on a mission. A Creative Mission. I know that we all have an infinite source of creative power and resilience within us that we can use to shift systems and disrupt the status quo. When you apply your creative power to your life, magic happens and prosperity flows. This concept of tapping into your creativity and using it to make a difference in the world is the missing piece for most people. You don't have to change who you are to make an impact. You can help people by being yourself, doing what you love, and sharing your truth with the world.

YOUR RADIANT WILDHEART SELF

The first step to living your Creative Mission is to get to know yourself and understand who you truly are. When you commit to honoring your truth, you can begin the process of embodying it and building a life that is aligned to what your creative spirit is wanting.

Most of us are born into a world with lots of expectations for us. We are told how we are supposed to dress and what kind of careers to pursue. We are encouraged to follow the rules and do as we are told. As a millennial, I grew up being told that the only acceptable path is the one that is "safe" and reliable. Be heterosexual, pursue higher education, get married, pop out some kids, retire at 65, and then die. Yikes! While we all grew up in households with varying degrees of appreciation for the arts, the medicine of honoring your creative spirit is one that will benefit you no matter where you are on your journey.

For as long as I can remember, I have always longed for so much more than what was offered to me. I wanted depth, connection, and meaning. Instead of waiting to be given a seat at the table, I decided to use what I knew to make my own table and chair. I then invited all my friends to come sit with me so we could have our own party. One that was way more fun than what we were waiting to be invited to.

Here's how it happened. With pressure from my parents to do something "safe" after college, I decided to pursue a career in art education.

Some of my artist friends told me that being an art teacher meant that you were a failed artist, but I didn't care. To me, there seemed like no better job than being up to my elbows in art supplies every day. I wanted a career where I could get paid for exploring my interest in creativity, and I was pretty satisfied knowing that even if all I did was make a difference in the life of one child, it would mean so much to me. So I went for it.

I didn't realize how healing it would be for my own inner child to teach art. I was still working on my creative confidence, so pursuing an art education career meant that I could learn alongside my students. From a practical perspective, I loved having permission to make art all day and think up experiences for people to create alongside me. But from a human perspective, training in the arts classroom prepared me to deeply transform lives.

When the doors closed, the "the rules" would go out the window. My classroom was an intentional safe space where kids could go to have their creativity fostered instead of stifled. It was the space that I always needed when I was younger, and my students loved it too. They would skip class and show up at the front door of my room to offer their assistance. Need help filing art? Cleaning paintbrushes? Setting up for the next class? It seemed like there was always a willing student volunteer who just wanted to be in our creative sanctuary for a little while longer. I took my role as the creative facilitator seriously because I know that even one careless comment from another student or myself could fracture a child's creativity for life. And many people are still walking around with these creative wounds that have been left unattended since childhood.

But teaching art was just one aspect of me living my Creative Mission. One day, I realized that I longed for more creative freedom than being a schoolteacher could provide. I wanted to make my own schedule and was inspired by all of the amazing projects that came through the school. So, I followed my creative impulse and left teaching to start a nonprofit. A business partner of mine and I created an organization to lead expressive arts and mural painting in communities. It was deeply rewarding work, but I realized afterward that I needed to be paid and paid well . . . so I started a business! I still consider art education to be the foundation of what I do. But now I can teach whatever I want, and I've found ways to make it my career. No one told me that I could do this. I truly made up this path as I went by following the **intuitive nudge** and the ideas that inspired me most. An intuitive nudge is that little voice that you hear in your mind that continuously guides you toward certain actions which will bring you closer to your healing or liberation. Often times, what your intuitive nudges are guiding you to do might feel scary or nerve-racking, but are also equally, if not more, exhilarating. Because there's more freedom on the other side of taking those intuitively guided steps that your spirit is asking you to do. You, too, can turn any fear into a turn-on and excitement if you lean in to all that's possible for you when you say yes to what your heart truly wants.

The first step is giving yourself permission to break the rules. I've always considered myself a bit of a rebel. It was something that I was shamed for growing up, getting in lots of trouble for speaking out of turn and doing what I wanted, when I wanted. Eventually, I channeled that rebellious energy into a positive force in my life. A source of strength when I knew I needed to follow my heart, despite what everyone else was doing. We all have this **Sacred Rebel** energy inside of us. It's the part of you that's a trailblazer. A bridge from the old world into the new. You are the artist who is alchemizing a new way of teaching, being, creating art, doing business, and building relationships. You tap into your Sacred Rebel energy when you are not afraid to trust your intuition and lead with your values to protect our planet and the people in it.

The old, outdated way of living was focused on money, capitalism, and endless exponential growth. All the power and resources were in the hands of a few people who weren't willing to reach down and help others up. Not anymore. We are shifting into a new paradigm where we are working collaboratively and generously to uplift each other. The Radiant Wildheart way knows that we go further together. And there's absolutely no time to waste. But it's not always easy to carve your own path, and that's why we're here doing this in the Wildheart community together.

We find ourselves at a pressing juncture. Our planet is on the verge of breaking, our economic and political systems are decaying, and we are coming to terms with the history of violence that is Western civilization and the Industrial Growth Society.[1] But I know it's us Radiant Wildhearts who are going to help turn it around. However, we can't do that until we're able to stay true to ourselves no matter the circumstance.

When you can own the parts of yourself that are unique and different, you will be unstoppable. Your uniqueness and all of your quirks become your superpower. To find your superpower, you first need to seek out or create environments in which you feel supported. And then, you can start to have a ton of fun unapologetically sharing your gifts with the world.

WILDHEARTS THROUGHOUT HISTORY

We come from a long lineage of Radiant Wildhearts who have been smashing through boxes and societal expectations to change the world and pave the way for our Creative Missions. These magical beings have harnessed their Sacred Rebel energy and creative spirit to make an impact in their own unique ways. Radiant Wildhearts are artists who are ahead of their time, which means they might have been initially misunderstood or unseen for their brilliance. And yet, their legacy is felt. Notice how the Radiant Wildhearts in the following list represent a vast diversity of gifts. No matter what shape their work took, they led with their creativity and a vision for what they knew was possible in our world.

Every single person on this list has faced adversity and backlash at one point or another. They probably doubted themselves and the impact they would have. But each of them pushed through because their desire for self-expression, liberation, and truth ended up being more powerful than their fear. They were moved by a deeper calling. By their Creative Mission. And we get to follow in their footsteps and pick up where they left off. If you are curious about any of these Wildhearts, I definitely recommend searching their names online and finding out more about their Creative Mission and legacy. Give them their flowers and honor the embodiment of their higher self and the impact that they had.

adrienne maree brown
Alexandria Ocasio-Cortez
Alice Coltrane
Alok Vaid-Menon
Amy Winehouse
Anaïs Nin
Angela Davis
Arundhati Roy
Audre Lorde
Bettie Page
Beyoncé
Billie Holiday
Billy Porter
David Bowie
Dolly Parton
Elliot Page

Freddie Mercury
Frida Kahlo
Gerda Wegener
Georgia O'Keeffe
Greta Thunberg
Indya Moore
Josephine Baker
Julia Child
Kiran Gandhi
Kurt Cobain
Laverne Cox
Lili Elbe
Louise Hay
Madam C.J. Walker
Malala Yousafzai
Marsha P. Johnson
Maya Angelou

Oscar Wilde
Patti Smith
Pedro Zamora
Prince
Ruth Bader Ginsburg
Sappho
SARK
Sia
Sojourner Truth
Sylvia Rivera
Vandana Shiva
Virginia Woolf
Walter Mercado
Whitney Houston
Willow Smith
Xiuhtezcatl Martinez

Expansion Exercise

Our first expansion exercise is to help you understand where you are now. Once you can locate yourself presently, you will have a better sense of where you want to go and grow moving forward. Your wildest, most abundant creative life is calling you. But before you can set your GPS toward it, you need to figure out what your starting point is.

Abundance Journal Prompt

Describe how your life looks in each of the following areas. This exercise is meant to be neutral and objective. If there are things you want to transform in your life, that's completely normal and that's why we are here. Be sure not to shame yourself. Just objectively describe the facts about your reality right now as you perceive it.

1. **FAMILY OF ORIGIN:** Are you as close as you'd like to be? Do you want to express more boundaries with any family members? Do you feel like you are "out of the closet" with your family? Can you be your true self around them? Is there anything you want to express that you haven't yet?

2. **CAREER:** Do you feel satisfied in your career? Is there anything in your career that you're longing to change? Do you make as much money as you want? Do you feel fulfilled by your life, whether it's through your work or outside of it? Do you find meaning in your work? Do you work in a healthy environment? What is your relationship to work, and does it feel supportive to you?

3. **LOVE AND RELATIONSHIPS:** What makes you feel loved? What do you love about yourself? Do you feel expressed in your relationship? Do you feel like you have a community with shared values? Describe your ideal partnership, if any. Describe your ideal friendships. Describe your sexual orientation. Do you align with monogamy, polyamory, or both? Perhaps something else?

4. **CREATIVITY:** What creative mediums are you interested in trying? Do you think of yourself as creative? Why or why not? When and where do you feel the most inspired? What are you most passionate about? Which artists do you admire and why? What fears do you have around being seen expressing your creativity or artistry?

5. **WELLNESS:** When do you feel the most nourished? Do you have any personal practices that you aspire to do more regularly? Do you feel that you move your body enough? Do you stretch? What foods make your body feel alive? What foods bring you comfort? How do you tend to your mental health? Do you see a therapist, or do you want to? Do you engage in any other healing modalities, or do you want to? Do you have any spiritual practices that are important to you?

Intuitive Creativity

Every single person on this Earth who has realized their purpose, and fearlessly embodied it, has one thing in common: the willingness to go on an adventure. And I don't mean the kind that requires a plane ticket or a backpack full of Lonely Planet guides. This journey is a wild one, full of unexpected twists and not without risk. But it's also so worthwhile. Because when you choose a life of listening to your creative spirit and aligning with your true values, a life of purpose can't help but manifest.

I'm a big believer in intuition and being guided by the voice of your higher self and **spirit team**. Your spirit team consists of healed ancestors, guardian angels, plant allies, animal spirits, ascended masters, and anyone else that's been walking with you on your journey. Your spirit team's role in your life is to help you live your Creative Mission, the reason why you came onto this planet. But, because you have free will, they can't help you unless you ask for it.

I want you to practice listening to your intuition and taking action based on what you feel. What this means is that you might not know where you are headed or why your intuition is guiding you toward something. That's 100 percent okay. What's important is that you get started. That you're willing to put your foot on the path and trust that you'll find your way. Keep saying yes to your truth, and your next steps will emerge and become clear to you. You may start this journey aiming for one destination but end up somewhere completely different. And that's perfect. That's how you evolve.

HOW TO BRING MORE CREATIVITY INTO EVERYTHING YOU DO

+ Ask questions.

+ Try new things.

+ Think outside of the box—and even outside the outside of the box.

+ Follow your desires.

+ Be brave.

+ Get curious.

When I first began crafting my Wildheart life, I thought that I would become a creativity coach. I was not expecting that I would be guided to mentor my clients in living their Creative Missions, expressing their truths, or growing revolutionary businesses and platforms. I arrived here after a wild journey of trying many different things and not knowing how it all came together. Eventually, I realized that I am the common denominator. And ultimately, it's my unique energy that I infuse into everything I create that makes it impactful and successful by my own standards, and magnetic for other Wildhearts who find my work.

Mistakes are where you grow.

﹥﹥﹥ CREATIVE PRACTICE ﹤﹤﹤
Intention Setting

It's time for your first creative practice, and this one is my favorite in my **magical toolbox.** Your magical toolbox is where you collect all of the practices, energetic or emotional tools, and healing objects that help you remember your power. Intentions are one of the first tools that I reach for in my magical toolbox on an almost daily basis. An intention is a sacred prayer you send out to the universe. It's a path of study that guides your experience. You are constantly setting intentions, whether you realize it or not. In every moment, you are manifesting with your words, thoughts, and actions. I firmly believe that all our intentions come true. So, you want to make sure you are setting the intentions that you actually want to manifest and getting super specific about your requests.

If you don't take the time to be intentional, you might manifest the wrong thing. Constantly focusing on your fears creates a self-fulfilling prophecy. If you look around your life and notice things are not as you would like, now is the time to set a powerful new intention so that you can use your subconscious to bring you closer to making your creative dreams a reality.

This five-step process will give you a quick morning practice that you can revisit as often as you like! Remember, all your intentions will come true. Are you ready to take your power back and set intentions for what you actually want? Let's get started.

STEP 1: **Find a comfortable seat.** Choose a space that feels sacred to you. You might sit in front of your altar or next to a window. Relax and get comfortable. Gently peer into the flame of a lit candle or focus your gaze on a tree or flowers outside.

STEP 2: **Ground yourself into your body.** Place one hand over your heart and one hand over your belly. Take three deep breaths and notice your belly as it fills up with air.

STEP 3: **List three things that you are grateful for.** Notice how the energy of gratitude shifts the feelings in your body.

STEP 4: **Call upon your spirit team** of guides, angels, and/or healed ancestors and ask for their support. Your spirit team is waiting to guide you into your Creative Mission, but first, you must ask for their help.

STEP 5: **State your intention for the day** as if it is already true. Like, "I speak my truth with confidence." You can also start your intentions with "I am." For example, "I am a divine beacon of inspiration for everyone that I encounter," or "I am financially and spiritually abundant." Make sure to be extremely specific and don't be afraid to claim exactly what you desire. Write your intention down in your Abundance Journal or set a reminder on your phone that periodically reminds you to come back to it throughout your day.

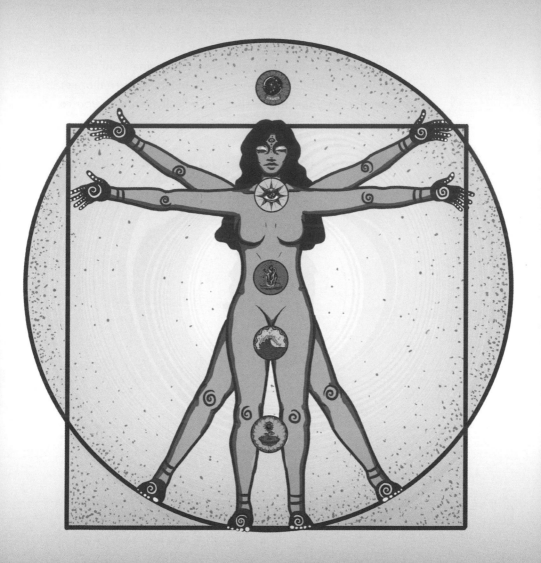

CHAPTER TWO

Meet Your Elemental Archetype

I've been blessed by the opportunity to help thousands of people express themselves through creativity, and over the years, it's become apparent that each person has a unique approach to how they manifest their Creative Mission. While everyone's journey is sacred, I've also found that people tend to fall into one of five different **elemental archetypes** when it comes to accessing their creative magic and living it in the world. Your elemental archetype describes your unique approach to living your Creative Mission. It will show you the strengths and challenges you'll encounter as you continue to create a life around your truth.

Since the beginning of time, people have used the elements for magic, alchemy, and understanding of our planet. Almost every religion and region of the world utilizes the different qualities and patterns of the elements: ether, air, fire, water, and earth. These are sometimes described as the classical elements, and similar systems have been found in ancient civilizations all over the world. Each archetype discussed in this book aligns with a certain element, the same elements that have been used to create the building blocks of the world in which we live.

They consistently show up everywhere, and I've found that they also show up when we begin to say yes to our true selves. I've devised this system based on thousands of mentorship sessions with creative, spiritual Wildhearts when helping them work through their creative blocks so they could unapologetically live their Creative Mission.

The elemental archetypes outlined in this book are the Mystic (Ether), the Visionary (Air), the Healer (Water), the Guardian (Earth), and the Sacred Rebel (Fire). While we are each dominant in one of the archetypes, the reality is that we all have a combination of each of these elements within us. We can choose to tap into different elements at different times to find the balance or strength that we need. While you are dominant in one archetype, the real magic is in alchemizing them all together to access the strengths and gifts of each element.

Quiz

DISCOVER YOUR ELEMENTAL ARCHETYPE

Please take five minutes to complete this quiz to determine your elemental archetype. Getting acquainted with the characteristics of your archetype will help you better navigate your journey as you step into your most expressed life as a Radiant Wildheart. Understanding each archetype's gifts, challenges, and unique energetic signature will help you to crack the code on your own blueprint for success. Not all of us learn and grow in the same way, but understanding your elemental archetype can help you chart the path that will utilize your natural gifts and better discern the areas where you may otherwise find yourself feeling stuck.

You can also take this quiz online at www.radiantwildheart.com/quiz, where you'll receive a full analysis of your Elemental Archetype.

Step 1: Circle your answers for each question.

1. **If you had 26 hours in the day and everyone else still had 24, what would you use the extra 2 hours for?**

   a. Ah, blissful! I would connect to my higher self by meditating, dancing, dreaming, and doing what lights me up.

   b. Whatever I want! Excuse me for not planning in advance, but I'm a spur-of-the-moment kind of person.

   c. I would work on my Creative Mission—talk about gaining an advantage, shazam!

   d. I would do something super fun and easy. I've got enough "to-dos" in my life and could use the downtime.

   e. I'd just chill and take the opportunity to catch up on *Tiny House Hunters* and fold laundry.

2. **You just stepped into a magical tea shop. Which blend do you choose?**

   a. The Limiting-Belief Zapper—release self-doubt and stop second-guessing yourself with this lemon-berry blend.

   b. Get Over Overwhelm—stop overthinking and start doing what you need to do with this invigorating matcha.

   c. From Shrill to Chill—relax, trust, and receive to sidestep burnout and renew your energy with this calming herbal combination.

   d. Boundary Bliss—unearth your ability to say no to what doesn't serve you with a balanced blend of sencha and ginger.

   e. The Action Activator—revitalize your drive and leave your doubt in the dust with a strong black tea infused with cacao.

3. **Fast-forward one year: You're chillin' poolside at a luxury retreat in Sedona, Arizona. Which book are you reading?**

   a. Something metaphysical, such as how to read the Akashic Records, the history of Reiki, or how to become a clearer channel for spirit

   b. A book about time management since I have so many ideas and not enough hours to implement it all

   c. A sexy, sensual compilation of poetry that activates all the passion in my heart

   d. A colorful book all about how to heal my inner child as an adult

   e. A book on social issues that matter to me because I'm ready to make the world a better place because the planet needs me

4. **How would your best friend describe you?**

   a. Open, loving, soft-spoken, considerate, and spiritual

   b. Creative, wild, lighthearted, and unpredictable

   c. Passionate, driven, focused, intense, and high vibe

   d. Sensitive, easygoing, thoughtful, and playful

   e. Logical, a good listener, grounded, organized, and calm

5. **Building a badass, super-creative life is all about _____.**

   a. leading from the heart

   b. getting creative and giving people what they want

   c. working hard and having a plan

   d. service, fun, and flexibility

   e. staying consistent and committed to your big vision

6. What would you say is holding you back from reaching your creative goal?

a.   Finding ways to share my spirit-centered work so that people "get it."

b.   My mindset and all the annoying limiting beliefs that pop up every time I try to do something.

c.   Lack of creative freedom, flow, and fun.

d.   Not having a proven game plan to work from based on my unique vision.

e.   Not knowing what my purpose is or how I can serve people.

7. If you were an ice cream flavor, which would you be?

a.   Lavender honey—ethereal and comforting all at the same time.

b.   Goat-cheese beet swirl—unpredictable AF.

c.   Roasted turmeric and candied ginger—wild and delish.

d.   Cotton candy with gold sprinkles—super sweet and hella fun.

e.   Vanilla bean—what can I say? I like the simple things.

8. What makes you *awesome?*

a.   I have no shortage of inspiration, and I'm happy to share!

b.   I'm easygoing, social, creative, and open.

c.   I have no shortage of passion and drive to make a difference.

d.   I'm empathic, intuitive, and wildly underestimated.

e.   I'm a loyal friend, and when I commit to something, I make it happen.

9. **Which of the following quotes feels like something you need to tape to your fridge?**

    a.   "A strong spirit transcends rules." —Prince

    b.   "We have been taught to fear the very things that have the potential to set us free." —Alok Vaid-Menon

    c.   "I'm no longer accepting the things I cannot change. I'm changing the things I cannot accept." —Angela Y. Davis

    d.   "Self-esteem means knowing you are the dream." —Oprah

    e.   "A generous heart is always open." —bell hooks

10. **You've got a long weekend and are planning a dreamy vacation to nourish your spirit and reconnect to yourself. Where is your soul calling you to go?**

    a.   Take me anywhere I can stargaze and remember my place in this vast universe.

    b.   I'm booking a night in a gorgeous penthouse suite where I have expansive panoramic views as far as the eye can see.

    c.   I'm headed to a festival where I can see all of my latest favorite artists that have been speaking the language of my soul.

    d.   This one is obvious . . . the beach! The cooling waters of the ocean always bring me back to center.

    e.   I'm long overdue for a camping trip! I want to unplug from technology, put my feet in the dirt, and be fully immersed in nature.

Step 2: Please take a moment to calculate your Elemental Archetype.

Write down the number of times you circled each letter. The letter that you circled most will indicate which of the following archetypes you are:

A: Mystic
B: Visionary
C: Sacred Rebel
D: Healer
E: Guardian

HOW TO UNDERSTAND YOUR ELEMENTAL ARCHETYPE

ETHER—the Mystic

Gifts: As a mystic, it is essential that your Creative Mission is spiritually aligned. You are a direct channel from spirit. You are comfortable living in the ethereal realm beyond space and time and have a natural affinity for accessing your multidimensional self. You know that your essence is so much more than what meets the eye. You are naturally gifted with psychic abilities and communicate with the spirit realm naturally. Your purpose in this lifetime is to be a bridge between the spiritual and the physical plane because you can see and feel things that others can't. I encourage you to build a Creative Mission that draws upon these spiritual gifts. Leaning into your spiritual essence and making it an essential part of your Creative Mission will help you finally find the fulfillment your soul is craving. If you're feeling like you desire more, it's time to honor your spiritual gifts and ability to see beyond the veil of what most people consider "reality."

Challenges: The main challenge Mystics face is that it can be difficult to put the incredible, abstract spiritual concepts that you know into language that others can understand. Sometimes it feels like your gifts are beyond words, and this can make you feel like you're an alien trying to learn how to assimilate on planet Earth. Sometimes, you may find that you don't feel fully understood. But that's because you are able to experience a depth that is truly limitless. Your work in expressing your Creative Mission is to try to simplify concepts and ground them down into the most clear and direct language as possible. This will allow you to reach more people who otherwise might not be able to grasp the multidimensionality of what you are saying.

Here's what your elemental archetype says about you:

+ You have a presence to you that reminds us of the divine oneness of everything in our universe.

+ You're naturally intuitive and connected to the cosmos. Your spirituality is uniquely yours, but no matter what it looks like, it's the place where you feel the most at home.

+ Your sensitivity is a blessing but can also hold you back. Remember that you are in control of your beliefs and of what energy you let into the divine vessel that is your body.

AIR—the Visionary

Gifts: As a Visionary, your Creative Mission has everything to do with reimagining the world as a more inclusive and healed space for everyone in our collective. You are blessed with the ability to see the bigger picture before the rest of us can. You're open-minded and quirky, filled with ideas

that are ahead of your time. You are a go-getter and full of creative inspiration, which means that there's no shortage of ideas for you to explore as you understand your Creative Mission. Your purpose in this lifetime is to paint the picture of a world that so many of us are desiring but can't envision yet. The more you can lean in to your ability to see it, feel it, and express it, the more of your fellow Wildhearts will be ready to jump onboard your mission and support you to create the world that you want to see. If you haven't spent time exploring how you think our world could be better, give yourself that gift while you work through the creative exercises in this book. Your vision is essential to helping us all find our most empowered selves in this lifetime.

Challenges: The greatest challenge you will face as you step fully into your Creative Mission is battling your own **shiny object syndrome.** Shiny object syndrome is where you have a tendency to quickly bounce from one inspired idea to the next. Often this results in incredible projects going unfinished and taking on more than you can handle. You are eternally inspired, and this is one of your strengths. But with it comes the shadow of learning how to navigate the world in a way that honors your energy and feels sustainable. We want you here with us for the long haul. And that means taking care of your energy and remembering that just because you see the whole picture, it doesn't mean you need to rush to the end point. Enjoy the process. Slow down. As a Visionary, it's important for you to remember not to start too many projects at once. Focus on one thing at a time and do it well. See it to completion. Be mindful of overfilling your schedule with everything that excites you in the moment. Otherwise, you might find yourself easily overwhelmed, without enough space to just be with your creative spirit and listen to the messages and visions that are coming through you.

Here's what your elemental archetype says about you:

✦   Your imagination is endless and something that you can trust to guide you. Don't be afraid to let yourself dream the impossible because that's the first step to making it real.

✦   Your excitement and enthusiasm are absolutely infectious. Follow your inspirations and share them, because it's your vision that moves others to action.

✦   You are naturally focused on the bigger picture. Your Creative Mission in this lifetime is about healing the collective, and you often put others before yourself.

FIRE— the Sacred Rebel

Gifts: As a Sacred Rebel, it's your passion and willingness to sit in the fires of transformation that allows you to make your biggest impact. You are truly a trailblazer, and because of this, it's likely that your Creative Mission is unlike anything we've ever seen. You are here to carve a new path forward, while honoring your roots and everything that this lifetime has taught you. You are truly a Sacred Rebel on a mission, and I want to encourage you to be willing to do things your own way. There's a revolutionary nature about how you show up in the world, and you get to give yourself permission to be bold and fierce enough to stand up for what you believe in. Don't have any shame about the ways you are different. Instead, turn the dial up on them. It's your uniqueness and fiery passion for your beliefs that's actually your superpower!

Challenges: While you are driven and motivated, you are also prone to burning out. If you are constantly on the go, so moved by your passion that you rarely take time to pause and reflect, you will quickly fall into a pattern of feeling exhausted. Another challenge that the Sacred Rebel faces is to be so passionate about your Creative Mission that you're willing to do anything to get there. This can lead you to burn many bridges and find that you are blazing a trail on your own. Remember, the truth is that we go further together. Pace yourself. Consider those around you as your accomplices and allies. We want to support your Creative Mission, but you need to make enough space for us to join you.

Here's what your elemental archetype says about you:

+ Perseverance is your middle name. You eat challenges for breakfast. This is amazing because you have a sense of self-assuredness that you *will* accomplish whatever you set out to do.

+ Passion fills you from your nose to your toes. It's what moves you and what inspires us to want to be in your energy. You have a conviction about your Creative Mission that we can all learn from.

+ You've heard, "you're too much" a lot. Many people don't understand your dynamic nature, but those aren't your people. It's your intensity that magnetically attracts those who resonate with your message. So take up all the space, but let others in to sit in the warmth of what you are creating.

WATER—the Healer

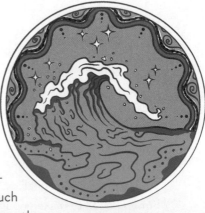

Gifts: As a Healer, your Creative Mission will likely involve holding a safe space for deep emotions. This is because you have high emotional intelligence and are very intuitive. You can't help but support people as they sort through what's coming up in their hearts. This is your gift and contribution to the world, so be proud of it! Much of the work that you do will likely draw from the experiences your inner child moved through. So explore those parts of yourself that you may have felt called to bury into the shadows, because there is actually a resiliency in those wounds once you let them out to breathe. There are many people in the world who are also called to heal themselves, and your way of being provides the blueprint for how they too can build a life around their desire to move beyond trauma and into a place of thriving.

Challenges:

As you step into your Creative Mission, you may feel pressure to do and accomplish a lot. But, for you especially, it's important that you give yourself enough space to flow and tend to your own healing journey. This is where you will source much of the wisdom that you share with others. While your emotions hold the key to your resiliency, be mindful of being overtaken by them. Sometimes when we feel so much, we can get stalled in negative feelings for months or years. Your goal needs to be to feel and heal what comes up. Never tell yourself that you're too sensitive or too emotional. Give yourself time to process your own emotions so that you don't stall out in them by leaving them unaddressed. And if you get stuck, reach out. Call upon your support team of friends, community, and mental health professionals whenever you are feeling blue to prevent you from entering a prolonged state of depression. Let your emotions be your teacher, but don't let them steer the ship.

Here's what your elemental archetype says about you:

✦ You're empathic, naturally intuitive, and the best listener. People love you for your chill vibes.

✦ If you tap into your power, you have the ability to be the cooling and calming voice or reason when others are overtaken by intense emotions.

✦ You are sensual and wildly creative. Let yourself flow and play with these aspects of your nature to find the lightness in an otherwise intense healing journey.

EARTH—the Guardian

Gifts: As a Guardian, you are driven by your values and your Creative Mission is naturally in service to empowering all beings to be happy and free. You care about the planet, its people, and animals. You put others before yourself. One of the things I love most about the Guardian is how grounded and reliable you are. You hold your creations to a high standard, and everything that you do is infused with a sense of thoughtfulness and care. People see you as someone they can rely on. They look to you for leadership, and they trust you to have their best interests at heart with good reason. Guardian, thank you so much for your selfless service. It's exactly why we need you to share your Creative Mission and bring the change that only you can.

Challenges: The biggest thing that holds the Guardian back can be summarized as perfectionism. You hold yourself to such a high standard that sometimes it takes you what feels like ages to actually share what it is that you've been creating. You might find that you rarely feel ready to share your work, or even to get started. You've been dreaming of something and holding yourself to such an impossibly high standard that you rarely seem to notice just how powerful you are. Know how much we want to see what you are creating, Guardian, and remember that the only way you will ever feel ready is to just go for it. Let things be messy and perfectly imperfect. There are so many people sharing their work with hardly an iota of the care and heart that you have. If they can do it, you can too. We need your Creative Mission, and we need someone like you to step up and serve. Jump and your wings will appear!

Here's what your elemental archetype says about you:

- ✦   You're the chill, grounded friend that people come to when they need a dose of peace and a shoulder to cry on.

- ✦   You truly care about the world and your community. You are naturally someone who leads with your values and has a strong sense of personal ethos.

- ✦   You sometimes doubt yourself and your power. But the rest of the world is waiting on the edge of their seat for you to claim your Creative Mission because we love the way you show up so much!

What's provided here is just a brief overview of all the archetypes. In each chapter you are going to find out how your archetype relates to the specifics of your Creative Mission. While you might be more dominant in one archetype, to truly embrace your most creative life, you get to alchemize the energy of all of them. We have all of these elements inside of us. Continue to learn about each archetype so you can find out how you fit into all of their strengths and challenges. The real work is in integrating and balancing out your dominant archetypal energy with the other elements. When you do, you'll fast-track your Creative Mission and move through your challenges with so much more guts and grace.

YOUR ELEMENTAL ARCHETYPE AND YOUR CREATIVE MISSION

Understanding your elemental archetype will help you know exactly what your strengths and challenges are when it comes to living your Creative Mission here on planet Earth. Before you were born, your spirit said yes to a very specific Creative Mission that will uplift human consciousness and help heal the planet. Your sacred Creative Mission allows you to play a part in shifting humanity into a direction of sustainability, creativity, and inclusivity. Understanding and integrating your elemental archetype into your life will help you get there. When you know how you operate and how you are designed, you can better understand and navigate any potential self-sabotage before it shows up.

The truth is that manifesting your Creative Mission is going to bring up all of your stuff—your wounds and any lingering scarcity mentality that you need to work through. When you say yes to your big Creative Mission, you are also saying yes to doing the healing work necessary in order for you to fully live into your power. This is a beautiful opportunity and one of the most positive aspects of living your Creative Mission, because otherwise, these same challenges might hinder you from manifesting your greatness for the rest of your life.

AN ELEMENTAL APPROACH TO MANIFESTATION

When you work with the elements in a specific order, you can manifest your Creative Mission, turning a divinely inspired idea into something that is real and tangible, and exists here on Earth.

Everything you create in your life follows this elemental process, which can begin to inspire and inform your actions as you move through the stages of manifestation and make your Creative Mission a reality from the ether to the earth.

Here's how it works:

Start in the *Ether*

This is the spirit space where ideas float around waiting to find their match. When you get a download, you've captured an insight from the ether.

Breathe life & voice into your vision with *Air*

Use your voice to express your idea and make it feel more real. Communicate your dreams and desires with words so that you can pave a purposeful path to turn them into reality.

Take action with the help of the *Fire*

Call upon your passion, ambition, and drive to enliven your vision and do what it takes to make your vision into something tangible.

Let your emotions flow like *Water*

You can swim in acceptance or turn back toward the shores, but there are gifts and healing available to you when you let water awaken the emotions that come alongside creation.

Root it down into the *Earth*

This is where things get real. Where you plant your vision like a seed and examine how you can create deeper, grounded roots. Your Creative Mission will eventually bloom into a gift that we all get to be positively impacted by.

Working with the elements is a fun and effective way to understand your unique approach to living your Creative Mission. If you want to learn more about the elemental process of manifestation and your archetype, visit www.radiantwildheart.com/gifts for lots of additional resources. Keep your eyes peeled for the Archetype Spotlights throughout the book, and have lots of fun learning about yourself so you can express your true nature through your creativity.

PART II

Embrace Your
Inner Artist

IT'S TIME TO MEET YOUR INNER ARTIST

Your inner artist is the creative genius that lives inside you and deeply desires to be fully expressed. Every single person, without exception, has an inner artist that wants to come out and play. Your inner artist has the ability to turn your entire life into a work of art. For most of us, our inner artist is probably a little shy and unsure if it's safe to be seen. This is completely normal. In fact, all of the most successful artists we admire have struggled with being seen in their creativity at one point or another. You now have the opportunity to stop running and get into flow so that you can finally embrace, reclaim, and embody your inner artist. Even if your goal is not to be a professional creative, unleashing your creativity is going to improve every area of your life and bring you more fulfillment in everything that you do.

Your creativity can absolutely be the most healing thing in the world, but without spending the time to cultivate your inner artist it will always feel daunting, confronting, and scary. In order to grow your creative confidence, you have to spend the time getting to know yourself. When you know exactly who you are, you can express your truth in the world without fear of judgment and shame. Your creative practices will regenerate you and bring you the confidence you need to become the Radiant Wildheart that you are. And that's exactly what this section will help you do.

We will start by uncovering what your biggest, boldest vision is. We will then dive deep into your own sense of worth so that you know on a cellular level that you deserve all the creative abundance that's coming your way. From there, you'll connect to your passion and remember your divine nature so that you can dance with the challenges that present themselves on your Divine Purpose Path. And lastly, you'll discover what your personal ethos is: the values that underlie your Creative Mission and the movement your inner artist is here to express.

Your inner artist is always alchemizing everything that you see and experience to transform it into something new. New beliefs, new actions, new creations, new brilliant ideas. You are constantly transmuting the information that surrounds you, and you have the power to create something intentional and influential with your experiences. When you embrace your inner artist and give them the space to flourish, your wildest, most authentic life can't help but manifest. Are you ready to give your inner artist space to play?

CHAPTER THREE

Vision

Remember How to Dream Bigger

GIVE YOURSELF PERMISSION TO DREAM IMPOSSIBLE DREAMS

When I told people about my dream to start a mural painting nonprofit, a co-teacher at an elementary school told me that it would almost certainly fail. She asked me how I was going to make money painting murals, and the truth was that I hadn't thought that far ahead yet. But I didn't let that stop me from talking about my dream of painting murals with children to anyone who would listen. I knew that it was time to take action, because I got so excited whenever I dreamed about my future mural painting projects. To me, it didn't make much difference that I didn't know how to start a nonprofit and knew even less about mural painting itself. I could figure all of that out along the way.

There was no blueprint, so I had to create my own map. I asked questions, did research, and talked with my friends and colleagues about my ideas. I reached out to mural painting project facilitators and made myself available as a volunteer, letting them know about my dream and wondering if they would be willing to help me learn in exchange for an extra set of hands for their projects. They were ecstatic to have the support and I was eager to learn. And my dreamy energy was a bit infectious. When I wasn't shadowing mural artists, I took classes and read books about community building and healing through art. While I was incubating my dream, I painted in the streets with as many people as I could until I learned enough to clumsily lead my first project. And from there, Green Seed Arts became a sponsored organization with nonprofit status.

I am my ancestors' wildest dreams.

After creating the nonprofit, I realized that while I had learned a lot, it was time to move toward a different, impossible dream. My creative spirit was calling toward building financial stability. I was tired of struggling and being stressed out about how to make ends meet. I had gotten used to being underpaid and I knew it was severely limiting my creative capacity. My soul wanted more. More abundance, more resources, and more creativity. I was 25 and hoped that by the time I was 30, I would be profitable and sustainable. Maybe even thriving. I really didn't have any formal training in business or entrepreneurship at the time, and I wanted to do revolutionary work that allowed me to be creative, fairy-free, and paid well. Some would say it was impossible. Others, including my own family of origin, looked at me and said, "You? An entrepreneur? Yeah right." Some of their naysaying got to me and instilled a little fear. But, at that point, my vision for what I wanted was stronger than any self-doubt. I said, "Feel the fear but do it anyway," and made a pact with the universe to show me the way.

When I hired my first business coach, I decided to put the entire thing on credit, as a gigantic leap of faith. I was telling the universe that not only was I committed, but I was going to make this money back and then some. I didn't have a plan B because I had to believe with every fiber of my being that what I wanted wanted me back. On a 15 minute discovery call, I asked the person enrolling me into my first business mentorship course if she believed I could make a full-time living teaching creativity. She told me that she didn't see any reason why not and gave me a couple of examples of people she knew that were doing creative work and thriving in business. I took that as evidence, believed it with my whole heart, and let it be all the affirmation I needed to say a full-body "yes." Soon after, I began implementing the strategies I learned from her to grow my audience online. And it worked, fast.

Almost immediately, I had 3,000 people paying attention to what I had to say and telling me how I'd changed their lives. Even though I was still terrified of being my full-spectrum self in public, people were seeing me shine my light and reflecting it back to me. This inspired me to keep going and keep sharing, especially when it was scary and hard. Even though most people in my life told me it was not a smart financial decision, and one I would regret, to this day I still look back on that leap of faith and consider it one of the best decisions I've ever made.

I've taken that leap enough times to know that I always find my wings on the way down. With practice, I've learned how to get comfortable in the discomfort of being a beginner and of not knowing the how. I can navigate my fears and insecurities with grace and experience now, because I know what I need to do to soothe my nervous system and lean back into trust so that my inner artist can keep moving forward. Fear is never a good excuse to turn back, but it is important information that helps us excavate, explore, and learn more about ourselves that can help us get to where we want to be.

One of my gifts is being able to see greatness in others and I can tell you right now, there's a greatness that lives inside of you. Your way of finding and expressing your vision is going to be unique to you. Your journey might not look anything like mine or anyone else's, and that's okay. It's yours. What's important is that it inspires you deeply, because that's what will keep you moving forward and pushing past the stretchy moments. The world needs your unique expression, your vision for what our world can be. And truly embodying it, and believing in it fully, is the only thing that will truly help heal your inner artist. So, don't worry if you don't know your end goal, what it's going to look like, or how you will get there. Just keep taking steps forward, enjoying the process, and trust that your path will continue to appear.

THERE WILL ALWAYS BE OBSTACLES

I learned early on that our obstacles can be our best teachers.

If you're going to live your Creative Mission, you have to be willing to take on risk, whatever that means to you. It might be saying the vulnerable thing, applying to share your art in a public space, or starting your own business. If you aren't willing to bet on yourself, you'll never have the opportunity to see what your inner artist is capable of. So many people are comfortably uncomfortable, unsatisfied with the world around them, yet unable to make the changes needed to come into alignment. But it doesn't have to be this way.

The key to creating your vision, regardless of if you know how you are going to get there, is to simply take inspired action. Let's start with a yoga practice, for example. In order to really master an asana or pose, you have to get into it for the first time. You have to create the shape in your body, even if at first, it's lopsided or misaligned. Once you are in the pose, you can feel where you need to adjust your body to be more comfortable. Perhaps move your hand a little to your left, or sink into your hips a little deeper. Every time you practice a certain pose, it will continue to get more refined. The more often you show up to the mat, the more you will feel the somatic remembering in your body and it won't feel as difficult or uncomfortable.

Understanding your vision is a process, and every time you take action, you peel back the layers of confusion which separate you from your truth—and your intuition. Because you've always known the answer. You know it right now. But in order to feel it, you've got to get into inspired action and commit to doing something, even if it's a small step forward, that moves you closer to your vision.

Expansion Exercise

WILDHEART CREATIVE DREAM BOARD

Your first expansion exercise is a classic assignment that is often used as a foundation for manifestation. I am including it here because it is important that you spend time creatively exploring and expressing the vision that lives inside of you.

Your assignment is to create your Wildheart Creative Dream Board. A **creative dream** is something that everyone has access to. It's a vision for your life that represents your hopes, excitement, and deep desires. It brings you lots of joy and aliveness when you think about it, and it's probably something that you would do for free. Remember, every single person is walking around on this planet with a creative dream, and you are no exception. Many people feel the pull of their creative dreams moving them toward something, and often those feelings don't ever go away. But most people haven't spent the time to hash out their creative dreams and get crystal clear on exactly what they are calling into their lives. When you know what you are calling in, you can begin to make all your decisions based on whether or not it will bring you closer to your creative dream.

Wildheart Creative Dream Boards give you the opportunity to explore your creative dream. It can be physical with magazine cutouts and a collage of pictures and affirmations, or it could be completely digital, such as a board on Pinterest. You could journal about your creative dream first before crafting your visual dream board if it helps you get a better picture of what you want your life to look and feel like. The most important thing is that you let yourself dream bigger than normal. In your Creative Dream Board, you have permission to wildly exaggerate your creative dream and claim everything you want and then some!

Seeing your creative dream all together in a visual format can be really inspiring. You can hang up your Wildheart Creative Dream Board in your sacred space or at your desk as a constant reminder of what you are working toward. Dream boards will help you manifest your Creative Mission into this reality by constantly bringing you back to your creative dream and reminding you why you are doing all this stretchy (but fun) work in the first place!

This Creative Dream Board project is open-ended. There isn't a right or wrong way to do this assignment, and it is meant to be an intuitive process. Your Creative Dream Board doesn't need to look like a traditional vision board that you've seen anyone else create. You can use found objects, pressed flowers, glitter, or anything else your heart desires. Whatever you feel called to put into the dream board is coming through for a reason. Don't question it or worry if it makes sense in the moment. Just let yourself create. Get out of your mind and into your body, letting your intuition and inspiration move you. After you've created your dream board, you can examine it with a more analytical lens and ask yourself why you might have made it the way you did.

Often when I ask people what they want or desire, they have no idea what to say because they don't allow themselves to take up space by talking or dreaming aloud about what they want. So many of us have forgotten how to dream, and this expansion exercise is meant to help you practice coming to the farthest edge of your dream. Give yourself permission to go there and beyond.

Now go make your Wildheart Creative Dream Board using this prompt: **What is your biggest, wildest creative dream?**

LIVING IN THE MYSTERY AND TRUSTING YOUR INTUITION

Being in a relationship with your intuition is foundational to expressing that you're a Radiant Wildheart. My life started to flourish when I really listened to what my **Intuitive Higher Self** was telling me. Your Intuitive Higher Self is the part of you that always knows your truth. Even when you might feel confused or unsure, deeper within you, your Intuitive Higher Self knows the answers that you seek. The more you practice listening to your intuition, the more clearly you can hear your Intuitive Higher Self speaking to you. When I followed my intuition and used that wisdom to live my creative dreams, I was finally able to stop trying to put myself into a box. I let go of what I thought success would look like and started doing things my own way to create a life on my terms and to my desires.

In order to really trust your intuition and the nudges you are receiving from your Intuitive Higher Self, you need to be able to accept the fact that others might not understand or see what you're saying as truth or fact. But not everyone needs to get it. There are some people who won't understand until they see you in your fullest, most iconic Radiant Wildheart expression. And there are others who will never get it or you. But you can't wait for others to understand you in order to live your truth. You have to be willing to trust yourself fully and let yourself create from the mystery of your Intuitive Higher Self. Get comfortable there and develop a solid belief in the messages that are coming through in order to make them a reality.

Your intuition might come to you in one or several of the following forms, or it might take a new shape altogether.

+ Clairvoyance—Seeing images or scenes. Sometimes a message takes the form of a metaphor, like walking over an extremely long bridge in a forest.

+ Claircognizance—A knowing. When you get an immediate intuitive download, like when you intuitively can tell that someone is not telling the truth or that you should apply for a certain job.

+ Clairaudio—Hearing voices. The voices most people hear are calm and even toned. Often these voices are sharing empowering messages like, "The timing is right."

+ Clairsentience—A feeling. Often this comes in the form of a gut knowing, an instinct, or feeling the emotions of others. It is sometimes connected to the tactical. For example, you might feel chills when you read a certain passage in a book. Or you might handle an older item and feel anxious.

Now that you are aware of these intuitive senses, you can pay more attention to the messages coming through your intuition. The way your Intuitive Higher Self speaks to and through you will be unique, and it's up to you to listen to how they show up in your consciousness. No two people are the same, and your intuition will be a very personal skill that only you can cultivate with practice and attention.

MEET YOUR INTUITIVE HIGHER SELF AND TRUST YOUR INSPIRATIONS

* * * * * * ✦ * * * * * *

"Follow the sparkly breadcrumbs."
— SAM BENNETT

Let the universe guide you. She is always showing you the direction you should go if you learn to listen. Your higher self is leaving you a trail of clues guiding you directly toward your Creative Mission.

Connecting with your Intuitive Higher Self is important because it allows you to have access to the wisdom of your future self, your inner child, and your healed ancestors all at once. Your Intuitive Higher Self has always been there and has never left you. You just need to cultivate your intuition so you can fully access them.

Keep in mind that you can turn to your Intuitive Higher Self for help and guidance at any time. It doesn't take more than a minute or two to receive Wildheart wisdom directly from them. Allow yourself the space to listen and follow these nudges toward loving yourself and the world as your true self, inherently divine, whole, and complete just as you are.

When you hear something that resonates as truth, you will feel the difference in your body. You can tell the difference between when you are using your mind to figure something out versus when you are feeling something that you know is true. The more you practice this skill, the stronger your intuitive connection will be.

For me, I know that an important message is close when my body lights up with excitement and I feel a surge of energy. I almost immediately enter a dreamlike Visionary state (maybe that's the Pisces in me), and there's a part of me that just knows I need to take action toward whatever is moving me. This knowing pulls me forward.

Here are some of the ways you can practice listening to your Intuitive Higher Self. Try them out and notice what happens when you follow your inner wisdom. Sometimes intuition shows up as a feeling in your body or a rush of excitement or inspiration. Sometimes it feels like a clear no or uncertainty about a decision that you need to make. You might not understand why your intuition is moving you in a certain direction, but approach this as a curious experiment and be unattached to the outcome.

Take Notes: Take notes of what happens every time you listen to your intuition and take action accordingly. Does it seem to work out better or worse than usual? Paying attention to these subtle differences will help you increase your connection to your Intuitive Higher Self.

Meditate: Tap into your intuition by meditating. Meditating doesn't have to look like sitting on a special cushion for an hour a day. For most of us, myself included, spending hours meditating each day has felt pretty inaccessible. Really, any amount of time spent quietly observing your inner thoughts will support you in increasing your connection to your intuition. Create a quiet safe space where you can have a clear channel to tune in and receive. Whether it's for 5 minutes, 20 minutes, or a whole hour, carve out space to just sit with yourself and listen to the voice of your Intuitive Higher Self.

Study: Teach yourself about intuition by reading books and watching YouTube videos. There are lots of magical teachers who are leading programs that will support you in increasing your intuitive gifts (myself included). This is especially important if you are someone who identifies as highly sensitive. If you are naturally empathic, it's essential that you learn how to protect and clear your energy so that you can keep in the good stuff while consciously releasing the rest. If you're interested in a course about intuition, check out my six-week course, the Divine Purpose Path, at www.radiantwildheart.com/divinepurpose.

Use Oracle Cards: Learn how to read oracle cards to help connect with your intuition. You will find all sorts of messages and insights come through so you can fully see the situations in your life. There are so many fun decks out there, and I probably have over 30 of them. I keep certain decks out of their boxes and around my house so I can pull from them whenever I want a spark of magic from my Intuitive Higher Self. I almost never use the guidebooks accompanying the cards. Certainly, they are wonderful and full of such wisdom, but I find it to be a powerful intuitive practice to not use the books and instead rely solely on my intuition. Giving myself and others oracle card readings has been a very affirming intuitive practice, where I've learned that many of us are struggling with the same things. It can feel so lonely trying to live your Creative Mission, but it becomes a lot less stressful when you realize that you aren't the only one moving through these challenges.

Practice: Your intuitive practice can look however you want. Start by focusing on at least one of these methods for a couple of minutes a day, and then gradually increase your practice to be longer. Eventually, having an intuitive moment multiple times a day will help you home in on the voice of your intuition. You can gradually incorporate more activities that draw upon the wisdom of your Intuitive Higher Self for longer periods of time. And eventually, following your intuition will become second nature.

You might have gotten a little too comfortable ignoring the messages from your intuition and your higher self. The insight you might be receiving is probably a little confronting. Making the powerful choice to take action based on the messages you receive can bring up lots of Inner Overprotectors. While it might be a little anxiety-inducing now, just know there is so much magic waiting for you on the other side. You are going to be rewarded beyond your wildest dreams when you start trusting in your Intuitive Higher Self. And the more you practice, the more strongly you will connect with them.

CREATIVE PRACTICE

Set Up your Inner-Artist Sanctuary

Nurturing a home that inspires you and lets you feel safe to explore your inner landscape is a creative practice in itself. You need a sacred space to go every day to connect with yourself, your art, and your intuition in order to continue to grow in your Creative Mission. This is the literal foundation of your growth. So set up a space that allows you to be a clear channel ready to receive divine guidance.

✦ Find a nook in your home where you can dream and connect with your creativity. This space needs to be inspiring in whatever way that looks for you. Maybe it's for cozy journaling. Maybe it's your painting studio, or maybe it's a sofa facing a sunny window where you can read. Notice what comes up for you as you complete this creative assignment. Do you notice fear, resistance, self-doubt, or disempowerment? Or are you excited to create a space that feels like a reflection of who you are and how you wish to spend your time? This is all valuable information for you to see exactly what you're working with when it comes to accessing your creativity on a more consistent basis.

✦ Be sure to tidy up any clutter. Keeping this space energetically clear will help you receive intuitive wisdom more easily. If you use crystals, keep them charged and regularly cleanse and clear them. Dust and vacuum so the air doesn't feel stagnant. Take care of your sacred space the way you would your own altar or temple, because in a way that's what it is.

✦ Beautify! Add any objects or artwork that inspire you. Perhaps it's a painting that you've always loved. Or perhaps it's your musical instruments that you want to reach for on a more consistent basis. Or maybe there are a few select books whose titles and covers activate something inside of you. Bring some intentionality to the space by decorating it and adding a splash of color. And when in doubt, adding a plant or vase of flowers always does the trick!

INNER OVERPROTECTOR

The Fearmonger

It's time to meet your first type of Inner Overprotector! They act so tough and mighty, but really they're just sweethearts, trying to do their best. The Fearmonger can't help but try to make you too scared to step out of your comfort zone. After all, it's super confronting to be seen and take up space.

What's the worst that could happen? Well, you could be rejected. Someone could throw a tomato at you. You might make a mistake and people could see that you're imperfect or . . . human? The possibilities are endless, and the Fearmonger wants to protect you by constantly reminding you of the worst-case scenarios. This prevents you from feeling safe and trusting your Intuitive Higher Self. The Fearmonger is an important Inner Overprotector because fear is at the root of all Inner Overprotectors.

You might be experiencing the Fearmonger if:

✦ You have a project on your mind, but you haven't taken action on it.

✦ You find yourself not speaking up even if you have something to say.

✦ You get panicked when you think about sharing your creations.

✦ You overthink and overanalyze, which keeps you stalled for far too long.

Tips for Dealing with the Fearmonger: Instead of thinking about what is the worst thing that can happen, spend some time dreaming about what the best possible scenario is. Remember when I said that all your intentions come true? Well, if you're constantly thinking about the fear and possibility of failure, you're going to create more and more of that which will definitely keep you stalled. Instead, take out your Abundance Journal and write down your best-case scenario. Make sure you write about what you want to happen, not what you don't want. If you consistently practice dreaming about what you want and getting more detailed about your vision, it will become exciting, rather than scary, to make it a reality.

Archetype Spotlight
ACCESSING YOUR UNIQUE VISION

 MYSTIC—Mystics are blessed to be getting inspiration directly from the spirit realm on a regular basis. Through the element of ether, you are tapped into a vast network of spiritual information and creative ideas that can help you to craft a vision that moves you on a soul level. It's up to you to choose which of these ideas you want to move forward with creating. Some things might be for you, and others might not. Check in with your intuition about what your next steps should be, so that you can keep taking inspired action toward your vision.

 VISIONARY—Visionaries have the natural gift of seeing the big picture. You know what your communities and environments are meant to evolve into before most others do. This gives you natural leadership qualities that are important to cultivate. But just because you see the whole picture doesn't mean you need to rush to the end destination. Take your time to enjoy the process and move forward intentionally and mindfully. Don't overwhelm yourself by saying yes all at once to everything that excites you, or else you run the very real risk of becoming overwhelmed or burned out.

 SACRED REBEL—Sacred Rebels understand on a spirit level that when the old way of doing things just isn't working, it's time for everyone to step up and evolve. Your fiery energy and passion is exactly the spark that's needed to bring this necessary change. Be open to feedback, and if you see something that could be improved, creatively explore how you might change it. Even if it's just for fun, it will help strengthen your problem-solving skills, which will in turn strengthen your ability to achieve your Creative Mission.

HEALER—Healers are oriented on healing themselves, healing their community, and healing the planet. Look toward areas where you can tap into your intuitive and energetic gifts. If what you're deeply desiring is intimacy and more presence in your life, then create that. There is no need for you to try and create the biggest, most grand spectacle possible with your art. Keep in mind, though, that when you're so focused on healing yourself, sometimes it's hard to look up and see the vision that's coming together right before you and remember that you're here for a reason. You will get through any and every challenging moment, and you will be stronger because of it.

 GUARDIAN—Guardians are incredible visionaries for the planet. You are very practical, stable, and reliable. We love this about you, and it's exactly why we look to you to lead us. But you need to stop being so hard on yourself! Your deep sense of perfectionism keeps you from giving yourself permission to dream. For you to access your creative powers, you need to feel safe and secure enough to plant the seeds of your vision into the ground so you can cultivate them to maturity. You get to nurture your vision from a seedling to something strong that can stand on its own, which will take as long as it takes. But when the time comes that it's your turn to share, remember that perfection doesn't exist, and you are so much more ready than you've given yourself credit for.

CHAPTER FOUR

Worth

Abundance Is Your Birthright

It was a snowy evening in Massachusetts. I was holed up in my room on my college campus, struggling with a painting that I had been working on. In a moment of inspiration, I envisioned a colorful rendition of sunflowers, my favorite flower and a spirit symbol that represented me alchemizing my pain into something bright and beautiful. In my mind, I saw a bundle of sunflowers overlapping each other, pulsing with energy and swirling colors, lots of expressive lines and dimension. I could envision it so clearly, and I wanted to bring these flowers to life on my canvas.

I had inlaid the flowers with sparkly purple swooshes, my favorite color. It was giving a very van Gogh energy, and I was excited about the possibilities. Maybe I was onto something here. But, as I kept painting, it started to look less and less like what I saw in my mind. My technical abilities weren't where I wanted them to be, and I couldn't reproduce what I saw onto the canvas. I couldn't shake the feeling that this painting was terrible. After a few hours, I ended up walking out in a snowstorm and dramatically tossing it in the dumpster. That dumpster had been staring at me from my dorm room window, and eventually I couldn't resist the urge to just throw it out. Get rid of it altogether. I felt shame. I was comparing it to other art I had seen. Thinking that by this point, I should be a better artist. I was afraid people would see it and judge me as a fraud. A fake artist. I didn't want people to find out that I **still** sucked at painting. So I threw it in the dumpster and never saw it again.

What's complicated is now that I think about this story, I miss the painting that I made. Looking back, I remember it with fondness. On some level, I actually loved it. But I was afraid of what other people would think. That it wasn't worthy of being seen. That it wasn't good enough. But for who? There was an imaginary panel of art critics living in my mind, and I couldn't seem to escape them. That panel still exists in my head, but I've learned to stop caring what they, or anyone else, thinks and instead focus on what I'm here to create. I wish I could go back in time and retrieve that painting from the dumpster. Sit with it a little longer and ask it what it needed. Or ask my inner artist what she needed in order to love the creations that flowed, even if they weren't perfect or exactly like what I saw in my head.

On one hand, I knew at a fundamental level that we are all creative beings with something beautiful to share. On the other hand, I judged my own work, and myself, with the harshest eye. We all do. It was only after repeated situations where I broke my own heart making choices that didn't honor the gifts that I contribute to the world that I could see that it was never about my own talent or ability. My creativity blocks were actually about my self-worth. It took me so long to see and own it as my **sacred creative wound**. And now I know that it's a very common one that might be holding you back from being wildly expressed and fully free too.

There was a time when I was used to settling for less than what I wanted or deserved. I would compete for jobs at places where I didn't actually want to be hired, and unsurprisingly, they wouldn't even call me back. I often felt underpaid and undervalued at most of my part-time art-teaching positions. I stayed in relationships that didn't actually feel fulfilling for me. I settled for friendships where I didn't feel like I was treated very kindly or uplifted. I couldn't make ends meet in Los Angeles, and I was working around the clock and driving all over town to get by. I found myself asking my family of origin for help, which is a privilege to be sure but also an embarrassing, unpleasant one to go through for me.

I was used to letting people walk all over me in my personal relationships. I didn't know how to set boundaries. I never stopped to ask myself, *What do I want? What do I like?* Because I desperately wanted the approval that I never felt I got. I was a people pleaser trying to gain love and validation in all of the wrong places. I would abandon my own desires and needs in order to be what I thought other people wanted me to be. But that didn't ever leave me fulfilled. In fact, it just perpetuated this cycle of self-shame and self-blame. I used to feel taken advantage of, even though it was me who was the one who couldn't say no. I couldn't name my boundaries, and I didn't know that I deserved to have them. I didn't even understand or know what boundaries were, because from what I can tell, that's not a conversation that happens in a lot of South Asian families.

I was a sensitive soul with a fragile inner artist. My inner child was looking for more evidence that there was something wrong with me, and that I wasn't a being deserving of love, and I found lots of it. Every single rejection stung, only exacerbating the feeling that I was an outcast, doomed to be forever misunderstood in all of the spaces I was in. And each time, my sense of self-worth got increasingly chipped away, because I was basing it on what everyone else thought of me. Even when I got validation and approval, it never was enough to keep me feeling satisfied or to ease the pain I was in. I needed to feel it within myself first, but I had no idea how.

When I started my business, I was forced to address my self-worth issue head-on because in order to get paid for my services, I needed to see myself and my gifts to the world as valuable. Necessary. World-changing. I needed to be able to stand behind my years of experience, self-work, education, and growth. I needed to own all of the beauty that I bring to the world. I needed to stop pretending that I wasn't good enough or that I was still a beginner. I had to do a lot of inner abundance work to see myself as worthy enough to be paid well to do what I loved. It was like my brain was wired to see my own value at $25 per hour at most, and then $35, and then whatever I could get someone to pay me! But now I see there is no dollar amount or price tag that I can put on all of this magic. And nothing will ever change the fact that I am an inherently worthy and divine child of the universe. And so are you.

When I first started my business, as a business coach, I felt like I needed to imitate other successful people to be successful myself. I still wasn't seeing the value in what I authentically had to contribute, because on the inside I felt like I wasn't good enough. And in this case, I was basing my own sense of self-worth on how much money I made. One of my first business coaches was a multimillionaire marathon runner, so I thought taking up marathon running would make me more successful like her. Unsurprisingly, running is not my thing. I've known this since kindergarten when I would unsuccessfully try to make up excuses to get out of running around the playground. I joined her marathon-running program that promised to help my business, and I hated every moment of it.

But you know what *is* obviously my thing? Creativity. Anyone who looks at me knows it. It's been dripping off me since I was young. But I couldn't see that for myself because I was so focused on what everyone else was doing. But they aren't me! And none of what works for them would work for me. It was like trying to fit a unicorn-shaped peg into a square hole. Never going to work, and totally ineffective. I've had to unlearn a lot of "comparison-itis" and emulating everyone else in order to find my own voice. Now that I've had a taste of what life feels like on my own terms, I only want to manifest the Creative Mission that is truly mine. Because life is a lot easier and more fun that way.

If I'm being honest, I still struggle with a lot of these same thoughts and questions about my own sense of self-worth. Based on the hundreds of conversations I've had and years of academic study of the creative process, I have a feeling that may never go away. Most artists just know how to move through it more quickly with more practice. I feel comforted knowing that I'm not alone. And that a creative life is the process of continuously coming back home to myself. It feels like every day, week, or month, I find versions of myself that I had forgotten about and get to reclaim. Aspects of myself that I love and missed, like that painting I tossed or the dreams I put on the shelf. I get to revisit them again, from a new place, and add even more layers of wisdom and self-love. As I continue to live my Creative Mission, I find deeper understandings of my truth. And I embody it more and more. Each time, it heals me in a new way as I understand what it means to be inherently worthy and unconditionally loved by the universe.

I am now the person who determines what my time is worth, and I place a very high value on my time and energy. I recognize what a gift it is to be in my creative frequency and the ways that my presence activates people. It's been a slow process that I'm going to take you on in this chapter, filled with abundance practices that I'll teach you so that you can incrementally step up your own self-worth and radical self-love. We're going to start by showing you how to feel abundance from the inside first. And as you do, your outer reality will reflect all of that magic that you've been cultivating through your life and your creativity. This is key for your liberation journey. Abundance work is for a lifetime, and it starts with loving yourself. And when you do, you'll see that your life goes from black-and-white to full-blown Technicolor.

Abundance Journal Prompt

In order to trust your creativity, you need to understand on a cellular level just how worthy you are, overcoming mindsets and behaviors that reflect a fundamental lack of self-worth.

Here are some examples of how a lack of self-worth might look in your life. This is by no means an exhaustive list.

+ Accepting jobs that you don't like or that don't pay you enough
+ Staying in toxic relationships
+ Lacking self-confidence
+ Compromising your integrity

✦ Not speaking your mind when you have something to say

✦ Being a people pleaser

✦ Lacking creativity

✦ Allowing yourself to be treated poorly or walked all over

Answer the following prompt to begin this exploration: **How does a lack of self-worth show up in my life?** Be as specific as possible and examine all of the different areas of your life where you know you are not fully honoring yourself and your inherent value.

Now journal your response to this prompt: **How would I approach life if I had a fundamental knowing of my inherent divinity?** Knowing that you are always whole and complete just as you are, with nothing to fix. That your process is perfect and that you will, with certainty, live your Creative Mission in this lifetime. What would your life look like if you approached everything with this profound sense of self-love, trust, and worth?

THE SACRED CREATIVE WOUND

Our creativity is a very fragile and precious thing that deserves to be protected. But most people don't have any idea exactly what treasure is inside of them. When you are young, your creativity probably got fractured in one way or another. For almost all of us, except those who are blessed to grow up with parents who are connected to their own inner artist, our creativity gets stifled under the judgments and expectations of the world around us.

As I began to unpack my relationship to self-worth, I discovered generations of unhealed trauma being expressed in my own life. I learned a lack of self-worth from the culture I grew up in, which says I'm only worthy if I have a desk job and a steady paycheck. And from certain family members who wanted me to only be a doctor, lawyer, or engineer. From a homophobic culture that told me that something was wrong with me if I was queer. And from the education system that failed me over and over again because it didn't know how to make space for my creative brain.

All together, these patterns and experiences contribute to creating my sacred creative wound. The sacred creative wound develops throughout the entirety of our life beginning in early childhood. Yours is unique to you and composed of all of the fears, limiting beliefs, and perceived criticisms you've received and subconsciously or consciously hold on to. It's what keeps you from believing that you are an artist and that your work is important in the world. And it prevents you from feeling truly free to be fully expressed and able to explore your creativity without shame or fear. I know that I am here to break those patterns in my ancestral lineage, and I have a sense that you are too. It is sacred because every single step of your journey is absolutely perfect. It is divine. And important. Keep that in mind as you let in the light to heal where your creativity has been fractured.

YOU ARE WORTHY OF ABUNDANCE

Your self-worth is the knowing that you are fully worthy, deserving, whole, and complete exactly as you are. You don't have to strive to be something that you're not in order to be worthy. You don't have to have the perfect look or outfit. You don't need to change who you are or continue on an endless quest for "self-improvement."

But you can't attract abundance if you don't know you're worthy of receiving it. All of your Inner Overprotectors and limiting beliefs come back to your own sense of self-worth. If you are playing small, doubting yourself, or questioning every step you take, you need to address this glaring opportunity to heal your sacred creative wound so you can live a life that inspires you and keeps your creativity alive.

You deserve a life of radical joy. You were born worthy of your wildest dreams. Abundance is your birthright, and nothing will ever change that.

Expansion Exercise

EMBODY ABUNDANCE NOW!

A lot of people feel like money is the measure for worth or abundance. But there are so many ways that you can access your inner abundance without changing what's in your bank account. And you can do it right now. You can go for an abundant walk in the park, go to the spa, take yourself to the museum, spend some time in meditation. Begin to ask yourself, *How would I take care of myself if I believed I was worthy of everything I wanted?* And how can you do that right now, even if you don't change your financial situation? This is always possible in one way or another, and now is the perfect opportunity to flex your creativity muscles to see how you can create your desired feelings using what you've got available to you.

This exercise is meant to help you identify what it is that will truly make you feel abundant. Once you implement the tools from this exercise in your life, you're going to find that you become a magnet for all kinds of abundance, including money, but also aligned opportunities, more fulfilling love, juicy relationships, and wildly expressed creativity.

••

INNER ABUNDANCE ACTIVATION

STEP 1:   Calculate how much money you desire to make. Start with your basic expenses. How much do you need to cover your housing, food, monthly self-care needs, taxes, insurance, and anything else you invest in on a monthly basis? Once you have that number, pick another number that would make you feel abundant and thriving financially. For the sake of this exercise, this will be your desired income goal.

STEP 2: Close your eyes and imagine that you have reached your goal and the money you wanted is 100 percent guaranteed to land in your bank account. What are you going to do with it? How are you going to spend that money? How will your life change? What will be different about how you spend your time? How will your self-love and creativity practices change? Spend at least 10 minutes journaling your response, and keep writing until you don't have anything else left to say.

STEP 3: Reread your writing and narrow down the top three to five feelings that you are seeking in order to feel abundant. Most likely, you are desiring a lot more than just a certain amount of money in your bank account. You are craving specific experiences that you are holding off to give yourself until you hit an income goal. Define what those feelings are that you are waiting to allow yourself to have.

STEP 4: Create three to five measurable intentions that you can implement into your daily life that will bring you closer to these feelings, regardless of what's in your bank account. For example, stopping work at 5 P.M. every day so that you can focus on your creative projects. Visiting a local yoga or dance studio to move your body three times per week. Shutting off the Internet at 8 P.M. so that you can spend more time with your loved ones. Spending one hour per day journaling or working on your abundance mindset. Or making sure to do your morning practice before jumping into work for the day.

STEP 5: Once you know what your intentions are, commit to spending the next week following them. Consider them your new Abundance Guidelines. Notice how you feel each day as you take these steps to cultivate more abundance energy in your life. After you've followed your Abundance Guidelines for a week, decide if you want to keep them for another week or shift any of them to keep your inner prosperity growing and flowing.

Six Different Kinds of Abundance to Cultivate

There is nothing that can change how inherently worthy and valuable you are. You were born this way. And you don't need to compete with anyone else because there is enough abundance for all of us right here.

But your world won't start to shift until you fully recognize this.

Spend time in nature and stare up at the stars, the mountains, and the trees. Know that you are made of exactly the same stardust. You are as abundant as this entire universe.

Once you begin to recognize how abundant you truly are, you will start to magnetize everything you desire toward you. It's amazing what can happen when you stop trying to force things and instead attract them into your life from a place of trust. It might happen today, next week, or next year.

Try to stay unattached to the timeline, and trust the universe to bring you exactly what you need to continue stepping into your next level of abundance. Remember that financial abundance is only a small part of the abundance that's available to you. Money is only a by-product of knowing that you're worthy. If you heal your relationship to your self-worth, yes, money will be attracted to you. But so will lots of other forms of abundance. Let's dive into the six main forms of abundance that you can attract into your life so that you can recognize them when they show up.

Abundance of Love

At the center of what it means to be a Radiant Wildheart is the remembrance that you are love. And everything that pours from you can be an expression of the love that you have for yourself, your community, and the world. Self-love is absolutely foundational to healing your life and relationship to your creativity. And when you love yourself, you attract a lot more love into your life.

If you are giving from an empty cup, nobody wins. You are responsible for managing your healthy energy boundaries so that you don't burn yourself out. You need to give yourself the time to be present with the voice of your Intuitive Higher Self so you can embody your inner divinity. Learn to hold and nurture yourself throughout your continual growth and transformation. There will always be ups and downs. But the amount of love that you can cultivate will fuel your entire Creative Mission and help you keep going even when those pesky limiting beliefs begin to show up again.

Abundance of Healthy Relationships

We attract aligned relationships when we recognize our worth. When we feel unworthy, we tend to accept versions of love that hinder our liberation. You might find your boundaries being crossed or your feelings being regularly hurt by people you care about, including your biological family. It's so important to cultivate healthy relationships that uplift you. You get to choose what relationships you stay in and whether you want to exit environments that are not actually supportive of your mental health. We all need relationships where we feel safe, can show up imperfectly, and be our full human selves. If you don't feel you have that, it's time to go out and find your kindred spirits. I promise, they're out there looking for you too.

As you continue to live your Creative Mission, you will have many spiritual awakenings and creative breakthroughs. Make sure you are cultivating relationships with people who have an abundance of supportive energy.

Abundance of Magic

To me, magic is your magnetic power. It's your ability to attract and create the things that you wish to see in the world. Magic is your embodied essence, and an energy that flows from you when you are feeling fully confident, aligned, and clear about your Creative Mission. Cultivating an abundant mindset is the key to making practical magic in the world. To using all your gifts, strengths, and tools to create the reality you want. The way that you live, speak, and think will create dramatic shifts in your life. And sometimes, these changes happen very quickly when you finally recognize just how powerful you are. You can live in a world that feels inspiring and hopeful rather than scarce, or worse, desperate. But to do that, you have to be aware of your thoughts and know that you can choose ones that are aligned to what you want to create in the world.

When you are fully connected to your self-worth, you stop trying to force things and can let them come to you. Because you know you are worthy and that the universe will deliver for you. The first step is choosing to move beyond all of the insecurities and self-doubt and step into a new chapter, one where you recognize exactly what you are capable of and why you are here. Remember that your thoughts and words are casting spells whether you intend for them to or not. Start to pay attention to how you are thinking about yourself and your Creative Mission, and if the thoughts you are having don't seem aligned to what you want to create, remember that you can shift them. All of your intentions will come true. If you can get clear in your intentions, you'll start to create magic everywhere you go.

Abundance of Pleasure

Pleasure practices are essential to keep an abundant mindset. I define *pleasure* as anything that makes you feel good. I have to regularly remind myself to take more time to lean into pleasure, whether that means incorporating an extra self-care practice or intentionally taking a break to find a way to celebrate all of the yummy feelings in my life. Pleasure also includes finding ways to incorporate more fun and ease in your process.

An easy and accessible way that I find pleasure is by listening to some of my favorite music from my teenage years, or even simply finding a few minutes to touch my skin and connect to my breath. You can make every experience in your life a little more blissful and pleasurable. And when you bring these feelings into every day as often as possible, you naturally cultivate an abundant and positive mindset that helps you hold everything you have on your plate and more.

Cultivating your pleasure practice is one of the best ways to get better at receiving anything, from love to money to opportunities. Being able to receive more pleasure in today's world is a radical act of liberation and self-love, especially when we receive so many messages telling us that life is about working hard and personal sacrifice. When you lead with pleasure, life gets so much easier. What small action could you take right now to make this moment even a little bit more pleasurable?

Abundance of Creativity and Self-Expression

Your creativity is a way of life and the lens through which you can approach absolutely anything. In order to experience more abundance when it comes to your creative expression, you get to first acknowledge all of the creative choices you make every day! Every decision you make is an opportunity to get a little more creatively expressed and aligned with your truth. Decisions don't need to feel so heavy; they're just choices. Every moment is an opportunity to choose your healing and Creative Mission. Let's bring the play and wild self-expression back into your life so that you dance through it with spontaneous and intuitive creativity.

Abundance of Money

The idea that money is supposed to be hard and a struggle is an old myth. The truth is that in order to make an abundance of money, you do not have to sacrifice everything that makes you, *you*. You can invite in more financial abundance without abandoning your values and everything that makes you unique. Money is simply an amplifier. And with someone like you, who is so heart-centered and committed to creating a positive change, the world will benefit when you have more money and resources. Nobody wins if you are feeling scarce, anxious, and spread thin. You deserve to thrive, and when you do, you'll use those financial resources to improve the world around you and uplift the people and causes you believe in. When you give value, you'll receive value. When you cultivate your own creative energy and live in alignment with your inner artist, a flow of abundant money is the natural next step.

INNER OVERPROTECTOR
The Comparer

It's time to meet another Inner Overprotector! I'm excited to introduce you to the Comparer. Your Comparer is always checking out other people and comparing your journey to theirs. The Comparer believes that everyone else is doing things better than you are, which leads you to not even bother to try. If you are focusing on everybody else, then you don't have to look inward at yourself and what might be coming up for you. This is a strategy the Comparer uses to protect you from facing yourself and your insecurities.

The Comparer shows up when you find yourself feeling a little jealous or telling yourself that your own ideas aren't as valuable or worthy of being explored as others. So you look everywhere for evidence that proves you right.

What I want you to understand is that your unique gifts together make for a story that no one else can tell. And the world really needs your story, not some fake version of you pretending to be someone else.

You might be experiencing the Comparer if:

+ You lurk on other people's social media pages and ultimately don't feel good about yourself afterward.

+ You make up stories about other people's successes and feel like you don't have what it takes to accomplish your own version of success.

+ You're always looking for other people to teach you, and you don't see yourself as competent or an equal.

+ You don't think your ideas are worthy or valuable of being explored so you look for evidence to prove you right.

Tips for Dealing with the Comparer: Instead of comparing yourself to others, can you see their success as evidence that you too could accomplish your Creative Mission? The people you are comparing yourself to are actually likely inspirations for you in one way or another. And the truth is that you are not in competition because there is an abundance of opportunities for all of us. In your Abundance Journal, begin to unpack the qualities that they have that you wish to see in yourself. If you can see it in them, chances are those same qualities are in you too. Their success does not mean that you can't also accomplish great things. If anything, it's proof of concept that there's a space and need for your unique magic, once you fully embody it.

See what it feels like to be supportive and uplifting to those you compare yourself to. Celebrate their success as you would your own, and you might find a comrade that you can collaborate and build with instead of a competitor, which feels *much* better.

Extra-Credit Assignment: Keep a running list of all the limiting beliefs, negative thoughts, or critical self-reflections that pop into your head as you tap into your worth this week.

Every time you hear the doubtful and fearful voices of your Inner Overprotector, write down what the thought is specifically. Keep this list on a notepad in your phone so you can update it in real time. At the end of the week, assess the fears that are coming up for you. Journal about them by finishing this sentence: "What I'm making this mean is . . ." Allow yourself to separate from these fears by reframing and transforming them into self-loving truths instead.

Archetype Spotlight

FINDING YOUR WAY TO ABUNDANT SELF-LOVE

 MYSTIC—On some level, ethereal people recognize that they are inherently and inextricably connected to the divine. From a spiritual perspective, you know you are rich beyond all measure. You recognize the soulful divinity in others as well. However, here on this earthly realm, your sense of worth is a bit fragile. You might feel easily wounded and challenged by earthly struggles like dealing with money or taxes. Don't forget you can always call on your spirit team and divine support to help you remember your inner abundance in those moments where you might not feel worthy.

 VISIONARY—Since you are usually focused on the collective and on the bigger picture, it's important for you airy people to slow down and tend to your inner garden. You take on so much, have lots of ideas you move forward with, and as a result you might find yourself regularly overwhelmed. What would it look like for you to recognize that you are already doing enough? That you don't need to accomplish more to prove yourself to anyone? There's already an abundance of magic in your life. Try to slow down and spend time with yourself to be present to it. Leave plenty of empty space in your calendar to be in flow and unscheduled. You deserve it. You're worth it.

 SACRED REBEL—One thing that you have an abundance of is passion. When you are aligned with what you are passionate about, you are so in your power. When you speak your truth, you find that sense of confidence that makes you so magnetic. Your message is needed, and you are the trailblazer who is going to lead the rest of us to step outside of tradition and create the world as we wish to see it. Just make sure you don't get lost in your own intensity and steamroll those around you in the process. Uplift them instead. Remember that we go further together, so use all of that fiery passion to bring us with you into your Creative Mission.

 HEALER—Oh, you sweet and sensitive embodiment of divine love. You have been on a journey that's lasted lifetimes to remember your worth, power, and inherent divinity. As a result, you are powerful beyond measure. Like the ocean, you are both soft and cooling, yet also profoundly deep and strong. When you recognize just how much power you hold, you'll find the abundance of self-worth that you've been seeking. Sometimes this quest for self-worth will have you feeling like you're drowning in your own emotions. When you're there, try to find pleasure. Try to hold the duality of life, both your shadow and your light. Eventually, the more that you cultivate all of your inner abundance, remembering your strength will become second nature.

GUARDIAN—Just like our beautiful planet, you are a swirling vision of wonder and beauty. Just like nature, you are perfect because of all of your complexity and diversity. Remember, you don't have to be perfect to be worthy. Imagine a forest. In it, you may see trees of differing shapes and sizes. Some are small, others are big. Some may be missing a limb and others might have even been cut or scarred. No matter what, each one is beautiful and essential to the whole. Similarly, it's your imperfections and quirks that make you so **you**. Embrace them and, please, let us see you in your process. Showing us your true self is a gift. And you don't have to have all the answers to let yourself be seen. Your worthiness is so inherent, your presence is so grounding, that there is nothing you could do or say to make us feel anything but grateful for you and your offerings.

CHAPTER FIVE

Passion

Encounter Your Divine Gift
and Offer It to the Fire

"Set your life on fire, seek those who fan your flames."

— RUMI

Standing on my grandmother's balcony in Dhaka, Bangladesh, I heard the calls from Azan echoing over the city. It's an Islamic call for prayer, ringing out five times a day. I used to hear it at home when a little electronic alarm clock shaped like a temple would ring in my kitchen. My father would stop whatever he was doing to heed its call. Walking up the stairs, he would face Mecca, and he would show his devotion for Allah (the Arabic word for God) by praying on schedule throughout the day. When I was looking for him, I would look to the top of the stairs first to see if he was praying, which he considered his form of meditation.

After 25 years and for the first time since I was one year old, I was finally on Bangladeshi soil. I heard the call of the Azan, but this time was different—in my motherland, as it echoed as far as I could hear. I looked out from her rooftop, one of the only single stories left in that neighborhood, and saw buildings and smog for miles. Hundreds of temples called out the same call for prayer, with different people singing to remind everyone of their devotion. It was unlike anything I'd ever heard before, and it was a sound I'll forever remember in my heart.

Growing up as a brown, queer Muslim kid in Las Vegas, Nevada, meant that I'd never fit in. I wasn't allowed to do a lot of the things that other kids were. I couldn't sleep over at my friends' houses or be open with my family about crushes on boys (let alone girls or enbies). My family regularly told me that I was too Americanized, as I had very little interest in hanging out with the other Muslim or South Asian kids that I knew. I couldn't really be open about who I was with them, or else it would get back to my parents. I didn't know who I could trust, and I certainly didn't see a place for someone like me in the religion as it was presented to me. I suppose that even as a kid, I could sense the cultural homophobia long before I ever had the words to describe myself or my queerness to anyone. And for a long time, I rejected my culture because I didn't know where or if I fit into it. I rejected it because I thought it would reject me.

I remember being forced to spend afternoons reading the Quran with Auntie Shumps, a sweet old lady battling breast cancer. She was very nice, but the last thing I wanted to do was spend my Saturdays sitting with her learning how to read in Arabic. I would get bored reading a text in a language that I didn't understand. I was going through the motions to please the elders around me, even though it was obvious that I was disinterested and disconnected.

At Sunday school, I learned the traditional way to pray. Islamic prayer as I learned it was very specific. There were certain duas (prayers) recited silently and with an exact sequence of movements, like a moving meditation. It was the same way my father prayed five times per day. And his father before him. And all of my extended relatives and ancestors before that. That connection to my lineage is so beautiful, and I'd never want to disrespect it.

But as a queer youth interested in punk rock music and finding my unique self in the world, it didn't turn on my deep sense of devotion to spirit the way that it did for others in my family. It was beautiful, yet I never actually took the time to memorize it. I pretended that I did. When I prayed at Sunday school, my silent act of rebellion would be to just fake the motions even though I knew I wasn't doing it correctly. I would day-dream until it was time to go outside and eat doughnuts and play.

I hid my true self from my extended family. I would block them on social media, change my clothes once I left the house, and fabricate elaborate stories about where I was and who I was with. On the outside, I was a rebellious teen participating in a vibrant counterculture filled with art and music, while experiencing everything life had to offer. But on the inside, I was living in fear that if people found out the truth about who I was, they wouldn't love me anymore. And whether it was true or not, this fear dictated much of my life for so long. Even with a thriving rebel spirit, I felt like coming out and openly living my truth was a threat to my sense of survival. And I felt this way well into adulthood.

I'm not alone in this fear. There are countless situations happening at this exact moment of young queer kids who are afraid of what might happen if they are outed to their families. And their fear is valid. There are many churches, musjids, and temples of all denominations that state very clearly that being queer, lesbian, gay, bisexual, gender non-conforming, and/or sexually divergent is a sin and something to be ashamed of. In many parts of the world, you can be killed for it without repercussion. Now that I'm older, I can clearly see the hypocrisy of this worldview. But growing up, I internalized the message that I needed to hide my truth because it was shameful, and even life-threatening, to be different in the ways that I was.

Like many children of immigrants, the pressure to live up to my parents' expectations was strong. I knew my father's vision for me came from a place of both love and fear. He didn't want me to struggle the way he did as an immigrant in the United States. He wanted to rest easily knowing that his youngest daughter, and all of his children, would be safe, secure, and taken care of. I'd listen in shock as he told me stories of how he went from being a young student in a third-world country to fully living the American Dream, with a successful practice as a surgeon, a home, and lots of children and grandchildren alike. He continued to send money back to his home country to help lots of people go to school and get out of poverty.

He always worked hard. As a teenager, he would wake up before dawn to ride his bike to medical school because he skipped so many grades. And when he brought me intricately cut fruits as a snack, he'd remind me that his children would never go hungry the way that he did. From where I stood, a very American teenager who was practically failing out of high school and didn't possess an iota of the responsibility my father had at my age, his stories were totally unrelatable. Yet, I felt the weight of them.

As I grew up, I rejected the world before it could reject me. For a while, I continued down the path that I found myself on in high school. Partying. Staying in relationships that were toxic. Numbing out my feelings. Not honoring the beauty that I bring to the world. I was disappointed that others, including most of my family of origin, didn't understand me. I secretly longed for their approval and spent a lot of energy worried about what everyone thought of me.

The adults in my life told me that pursuing my creativity wasn't a real, respectable, or safe path, and for a while I believed them. I was disconnected from my contributions to the world because I was uninspired by what was expected of me—that is, until I started to trust my Creative Mission even if those around me didn't understand or believe that I could do it. Eventually, by trusting in my soul's purpose and letting my passions guide me, I started to understand that I was put on this planet for a reason. And that my contributions mattered—a lot. Now I look back at my life and love the fact that every job I've had has been rooted in creativity. As a kid, I didn't even know this was possible because I didn't see examples of people like me who were living their Creative Mission and thriving.

I never expected that my Creative Mission would lead me to come out to my family of origin as a queer artist. As a business and marketing mentor, I often talked about authenticity and encourage my students to be themselves in their messaging. Every day I was showing them the importance of telling their stories, yet here I was, leaving out a huge part of my own story. Although all of my friends considered me a queer spokesperson, I was still leading a double life with my family of origin. I had been afraid of what would happen if the news of my sexuality and queerness got back to them. Not just my parents, but also hiding myself from what felt like millions of cousins, aunts, and uncles because if one found out, they all could. I knew that I would be gossiped about and shamed for damaging the family reputation, so I internalized it all and told myself that it was easier to just pretend that I was someone that I'm not. The truth was that it was absolutely exhausting to live this way.

For a few years, I tried many times to come out of the closet and it just wouldn't happen. I would say to myself, *Okay, I'm doing it!* But the right time never presented itself. I eventually realized that there would never really be a right time to have that conversation. Coming out is messy. And scary. But I had to be okay with the mess and just say it. And anything that happened after that would be perfect because at least it was the truth. Whatever happened, my soul told me that I needed to live my truth.

It took me until I was 30 to finally muster up the courage and do it. I had spent years prior preparing myself by talking to therapists and healers about it. So, I scheduled a one-day detour stop to Las Vegas on my way to San Francisco Pride with my then girlfriend. Even though I was in my 30s, being at my parents' house instantly transported me back to being the closeted teenager with all those unresolved and complicated feelings that came along with it. One morning as I was leaving my parents' house, I saw the familiar image of my dad praying over the Quran with his prayer cap on. A huge swath of light was beaming in through the window around him. He looked up and said, "Come over here, I want to talk to you," and my stomach dropped.

I had mentioned at the dinner table the night before that I got bullied when I was in elementary and middle school, and apparently this was a surprise to him. He had said, "If you'd have told me that, I would have put a stop to it." I had gotten used to keeping everything from my family since a young age, so no, I didn't tell him that, or anything else, at the time.

As he waited for me to walk over, I realized this was it—my opening—a rare vulnerable moment. I didn't have many of those with my dad so I figured if there ever was a time for me to come out as queer, this was it. I sat down across from him, the sun now shining down on both of us, as I fumbled over my words trying to explain to him what it meant to be queer.

> Queer /kwir/ verb, noun, adjective. To exist outside of societal norms. To take the unconventional path in relationships and sexuality. Subversive by nature. Inherently connected with the politics of liberation for all beings who fall outside of dominant identities.

Keep in mind, like many Asian American immigrant families, my family is not the type to engage in authentic or vulnerable conversations about emotional things at all. I had rehearsed the conversation prior to that day with my therapist, but in the moment, all my practice flew out the window as I clumsily tried to explain what it means to be queer. After I shared with him my identity, he shook his head, confused.

"How can you call yourself that?" my father asked. To his generation, *queer* was a derogatory slur, and he didn't understand how I could willingly identify with it. He didn't know that this sacred word had been totally reclaimed to be something empowering, liberating, and home for so many of us. He was concerned that I would have a more difficult life if I chose to be queer. I didn't tell him that my definition of suffering would be to hide who I am and live a lie for the comfort of others.

Although I tried with all of my might to fight it, I choked up and cried a little. Identity work and vulnerability are difficult enough without the additional awkwardness of trying to explain your sexuality to your religious and traditional father—or any family members for that matter. As soon as I could, I bolted out of there through the front door. And for the first time in my life, I felt a huge weight lift off my shoulders. I could breathe.

I didn't realize that I had been silently suffocating for my entire life. I didn't realize how exhausting it was to hide myself from the world. What a heavy burden it was to carry, none of which was my own. It belonged to all of us. To all of the queer kids who are forced to lead a double life for fear of their safety. To all of our ancestors who couldn't speak their truth because they were different in ways that were deemed unacceptable. To everyone who sacrificed a life of love for the comfort of others but at the expense of themselves.

Now that my truth was out in the open, no one could hurt me with it anymore. With each person who gets the privilege of knowing the real me, my inner artist takes another giant step forward and my self-expression gets that much more room to breathe. Because there is nothing wrong, sinful, or shameful about being queer. In fact, it's the opposite. Queerness is beautiful, sacred, and revolutionary. And I'm going to love and represent my queer community loudly, as an act of devotion and reverence for all of the beings across all timelines who weren't able to.

Like many of my queer kin, I'm still coming out in new ways to myself and others. Every time I do, I get to experience that feeling of being in more alignment with my values. It connects me to everything that's divine and holy. But it's never easy. It's not all rainbows and unicorns. A lot of my coming out journey has been painful. I've shed countless tears for myself and others. And the more I allow myself to feel it all, the more I remember what truly matters. I'm committed to liberation of all beings in this lifetime. I honor the divine by staying true to myself despite what anyone has to say about it.

I get to live my soul's desire of being fully self-expressed, loved, and accepted as I am. But I've had to work hard for it and learn how to choose myself and my healing. And what I've realized is that by sharing my truth unapologetically, I'm being of service. I've gotten countless messages from queer youth and adults who are inspired by my story and who, too, wish to come out to themselves or others. This has been such medicine for me on my healing journey. It encourages me to continue to be the role model I needed when I was growing up. I would so much rather help other queer youth to live without shame than hide my truth for the comfort of other's homophobia.

I now know that there is a place for someone like me. I've found where I belong and what my purpose here on this planet is. It's so much bigger than anyone's expectations for me. I practice devotion in my own way that feels meaningful to me. It exists deep in my creative spirit, in my Radiant Wildheart, and I create it for myself every day. It's when I feel that expansive love within me, which transcends any imaginary borders of tradition or cultural expectation. It's infinite, and it's what drives me to fulfill my deepest calling here in this lifetime, to be of service as the full-spectrum expression of limitlessness I feel in my soul. I always want to get back to this place, where I feel at home within myself and as free as the wind.

It took me a long time to realize that I cannot be separated from love. And that there is space in the universe for every part of me, including and especially my queerness. My existence, our existence, matters and is worth fighting for. And this knowing connects me to something so much bigger than myself. It's the light inside of me that will never go out, no matter how much the world has tried to dampen my flame. Every time I choose to accept all of myself, and with a deep breath, I come home to the inner-temple inside of me. I stoke the flame that keeps my creative spark alive.

Teaching

IGNITING YOUR INNER-LIGHT
BY CONNECTING TO YOUR MUSES

In order to heal the world, you have to first fall in love with your **inner muses**. Inside of your creative heart, there's a temple of divine love where you can always go to pray. At this temple are your inner muses, magical intelligent beings that you can court and converse with to support you in finding that which inspires those flames of passion and aliveness. Your muses have a fairy-like nature and are so much fun to connect with. As you continue your journey of finding your artistry, you must continuously and intentionally stoke these flames, remembering and honoring the endless fountain of beauty, inspiration, and light that's always inside of you and surrounding you. The more you honor the beauty of your world and yourself, the more your muses will walk with you, bringing you divinely inspired ideas and the creative sparkle that only you can feel.

The first key to understanding and working with your muses and sparking those flames of passion is to learn to hold your creative process lightly. Hold it with sweetness and lots of self-compassion. There is no point in being hard on yourself. And when you are, your muses will run because they love to be adored and courted, rather than criticized or ignored.

Throughout your journey of embodying your inner artist, you will experience many challenges and dark nights of the soul. You'll want to metaphorically burn everything down and rise from the ashes. You might find yourself wanting to reimagine your life all together. This evolution is important. It's not starting over, but it's building on everything that you've learned to bring your Creative Mission to the world.

You might be feeling any of the following:

+ Lack of drive

+ Self-doubt

+ Low self-worth

+ Uncertainty about what is special about you

Don't shy away. All of this is normal. Allow yourself to be in the underworld, if that's where you are. Go into those depths to reclaim all of those parts of yourself that want to be expressed. Here you'll find what you are passionate about. Don't shame yourself for any of your process. Instead, utilize your sense of devotion. Call upon your muses to help you remember why you are doing this in the first place. That inspiration will keep you going. Practice courting your muses in those moments where you feel discouraged. Let your muses help you hold your pain and find the beauty in these lessons so that you can dance with your shadows as much as you do your gifts. Your sacred creative wound is where your wisdom can be found. And that wisdom is being gifted directly to you from the divine and from your muses to transmute into an offering to the world, a gift that only you can share.

Wildheart, as you connect with your muses and find what you're truly passionate about, you're going to meet and discover new parts of yourself, as well as old identities you may have forgotten but are ready to reclaim. Your muses will guide you to follow your own rhythm, and they'll whisper messages to you that you can no longer ignore. You'll meet your true self for what feels like the first time. But these aspects of you have always been there, longing for you to remember them. Let your muses guide you to those places. Invite them in and make offerings to them. They'll show you how to dance with all of the energy that's coming through you, whether it's blissful, ecstatic, or filled with grief. Each one of these emotions are fleeting, and you can choose to witness your journey and creative revolution with gratitude and even a sense of divine play so you don't get stalled in the heaviness for too long.

Underneath all the "shoulds" and "supposed to's" is the real gift of who you are. Reconnecting with your passion—that which makes you feel alive—will naturally show you what it is that you are meant to be doing in this lifetime. Allow the blessings to come through by releasing everything that no longer serves you and who you are becoming. Whether it's identities, beliefs, relationships, or patterns that have kept you from living your truth, you can begin to let them go and instead devote your life to your inner muses and the unfolding of your creative spirit. When you do, a life of belonging and true fulfillment will naturally manifest.

ON APATHY

The opposite of passion is apathy. This might look like discontent with your life, but pay close attention. These feelings are actually teaching you something important about how to live in a way that lights you up from the inside.

Apathy might look like:

+ Waking up in the morning and not wanting to get out of bed
+ Feeling like there's nothing to be excited about
+ Not wanting to even try or bother
+ Living on autopilot
+ Being indecisive and unable to take steps toward your creative expression

A lot of times we develop a sense of apathy when we are lacking an aligned community and feeling alone. I know for me, when I was a student in high school, my apathetic nature was a result of feeling unseen and misunderstood in my true gifts and creativity.

Your sense of passion is intimate and personal. It doesn't matter what others think about your passions and the things you are devoted to. You don't have to be discouraged if others don't feel the same way about those things. There will be people who understand, and others who don't. At the end of the day, your sense of passion has absolutely nothing to do with any-one else. It's a feeling inside. Cultivate your passion in your own way based on what feels aligned for you and what truly turns you on. Passion is individ-ual for each person, passion is pure heart, passion is intimacy with yourself.

Abundance Journal Prompt

What does passion mean to you? How do you define it for yourself? What does passion feel like in your body? What times or situations have you felt the most passion?

BEING TOO BUSY TO CONNECT WITH YOUR PASSION

For many of us, myself included, being busy is a coping mechanism. We fill our schedules with all sorts of things that hold us back from spending time cultivating our relationship with our inner muses and ourselves. The vibration of scarcity or not enough time can put us in that apathetic place where we just don't feel inspired anymore.

Take, for example, if you have a job you don't like that doesn't align with your passions. It can be natural to feel apathetic and discouraged, because you might be feeling a scarcity that you don't have time to do the things that truly matter to you. But know that even if you are in a situation that is less than ideal and filled with divine passion, you can still cultivate an abundant mindset that will help you both magnetize opportunities that are coming your way and see the opportunities that are right in front of you. When you are operating from a place of scarcity, you might cut yourself out from the game before you have even given yourself a chance to play.

We are all magnets for the things we desire. We can either take responsibility for changing our vibration, thoughts, and belief systems in order to activate that magnet for the things that we want, or we can continue cultivating and perpetuating more and more scarcity and lack.

You can shift your vibration to focus on the things you feel grateful for. To pay attention to the abundance that you do have. To sit with yourself and your longing. To connect with your muses and creativity in small bursts so that you can feel the passion that lives inside of you and build on it. You can bring more of this presence into every area of your life, remembering that abundance is everywhere. And you don't necessarily need to abandon your current situations; instead, you can choose to go within and find that passion. To pursue your sense of fulfillment in other areas that will make everything that you do feel easier and your overall mindset feel a lot more inspiring. If you can't yet change your situation, you can at least change your vibration around it.

AWAKEN YOUR INNER MUSES

There is a divine space that lives beyond our minds, beyond analytical reasoning and trying to "figure everything out." That's where your inner muses love to play.

In order to really find flow, approach your Creative Mission with a sense of passion and trust in that divine space beyond what you know right now. When you understand that you are an embodiment of everything that is sacred and holy, you will know that you are always supported.

The universe wants you to live your Creative Mission and supports you in making it a reality. You can surrender your fear and burn away the illusions that are not the truth of who you are. What will remain is your gift, your offering to the world.

It's natural to question yourself. But your connection to your own divinity will help you navigate whatever challenges life offers. One amazing resource that you always have access to are your inner muses. Cultivate a relationship with them to lift you up as you embody your Creative Mission.

Your muses love to be adored with offerings and romance. Know that when you are loving up on them, you are loving up on yourself. You are nurturing your creative spirit and tending to a lifelong relationship that will truly support you. Awakening your inner muses means cultivating that sense of devotion for your future self, despite any doubts or limiting beliefs. You don't have to overthink it. Just let yourself dance with the energy that moves you toward your inspirations.

Practice

COURTING YOUR MUSES
AND RECEIVING THEIR GUIDANCE

Your muses will show up even more strongly for you if you intentionally cultivate a space that invites them into your life and honors the many gifts that they have to share with you. You can connect with your inner muses by making offerings to them, writing to them, taking yourself on artist dates, and taking the time to bring more beauty into your everyday routine. When you feel that spark of inspiration, or a divinely guided idea that you keep hearing, those are your muses trying to communicate with you. The more you practice communicating with your muses, the more you can let your relationship with them help you make divinely guided decisions that will bring you closer to your Creative Mission and fullest expression of life.

Here is a quick and simple process for how you can connect to your inner muses and receive their guidance. This practice is for anyone, regardless of faith. What I love about this practice is that it doesn't have to take more than a minute or two. Whenever you feel unclear about what step you should take or are spiraling in your mind about the many choices you have, you can always call upon your muses and receive a quick and intuitively guided answer.

To connect to your inner muses, follow these steps:

1. Get clear on your question and find a sacred space for you to go inward.

2. Close your eyes and ask your question aloud or nonverbally.

3. Wait and listen. Wait for as long as it takes.

4. Receive your answer. Make sure the answer that you get comes from your body wisdom and not from your mind. You should be able to feel the difference. If your answer comes from your rational mind and feels analytical, keep listening. Eventually you will hear an answer that is your truth. It might feel more emotional, and it will resonate with your essence. Somatically you'll feel it lower in your body than your head, like in your heart space or gut. And it will just feel right.

5. Take action according to this answer, trust it, and note the result.

No matter where you are, you can always find a way to be with your muses. Whatever has you feeling stuck is energy longing to be moved. Your muses might inspire you to move that energy through dance, art, journaling, or even screaming into a pillow. There is wisdom available to you that lives outside of your rational mind. It's found in your creative spirit and when you connect to your muses, you will find that aliveness that reminds you of who you truly are. And you can offer all of those illusions—the limitations and the self doubt that are so heavy to carry with you—to the fire. From the ashes, you'll find that lightness and remember the version of yourself that knows your magic and is not afraid to offer it to the world as a sacred gift that is meant to be shared.

INNER OVERPROTECTOR
The Robot

Our next Inner Overprotector is the Robot. The Robot goes through the motions and is stuck in a routine that rarely changes. The Robot is okay with very slow growth and following commands. Even though deep down there's a desire for more, they feel more comfortable just doing what they are told. The Robot is comfortably uncomfortable and often too apathetic to do anything about it.

The Robot encourages you to go along with everything as is, without stretching toward the things that turn you on and make you feel passionate, whether it's creativity, love, or travel. You might be experiencing the Robot if:

+ You find yourself saying that you're bored often.

+ Nothing seems to excite you or make you feel joy.

+ You are having a hard time connecting with your inspirations.

+ You're stuck but feel powerless to make change.

+ You can't see the opportunities coming your way and aren't looking for them.

Tips for Dealing with the Robot: Tap into your passion in order to override the Robot and remember that you are alive. Spend time journaling about why you feel that it's a safer or more acceptable choice to follow the motions rather than pursue your creative dream. Incorporate five-minute creativity breaks and find an accountability buddy to make sure that you take at least one per day or week. The more you can break the monotony and lead with pleasure and passion, the more you will find that spark again.

Archetype Spotlight

ACCESS DIVINE WISDOM AND LET IT MOVE YOU

 MYSTIC—Sufi poets are often called Mystics. And it's no coincidence that you, as an ethereal being, naturally identify with the side of yourself that is mystical and connected to the inherent oneness of all that is. You are naturally a multidimensional being and are actually more at home in the spirit realm than you might be on Earth! Just be sure to protect your energy, because not all beings out there are going to be helpful for you. If you decide to explore the spirit realm more, make sure to prepare by doing lots of clearing and boundary work. In order to avoid feeling lost floating in the ether, make sure that you ground your mysticism with something tangible here on Earth.

 VISIONARY—Air beings have millions of ideas coming at them in every moment, and they often forget to slow down and check in with their spiritual desires. Become more consistent in spending at least a little bit of time being present with yourself. Also, don't forget to add in lots of pleasure. Incorporating some stillness and pleasure will make a huge difference in your mindset, so you can finally step more fully into your big, beautiful vision.

SACRED REBEL—Passion is your strong suit, and one of the main words I would use to describe you. You naturally live your life with a sense of fire and a commitment to keeping those flames alive. When you embrace this aspect of yourself, you are a transformer of worlds. Sometimes your passionate energy might be a little intense for people, especially those who are not as quick to welcome change and transformation. But those aren't your people. Your fire and passion is a gift, and it ignites those around you. Study the things that light you up, and learn how to harness that energy and passion in a positive and constructive way so you don't accidentally burn down the house.

 HEALER—Water beings flow with the waves of life. You can be shapeless and formless, or you can adapt to wherever you are. You have the power to choose what type of shape you want to take. There may be times when you are moving through a dark night of the soul, but remember that everything that comes up for you on your Divine Purpose Path is meant for your healing. Your purpose in life is to heal yourself, and by doing that you will heal others. Your connection to your passion begins with your intentions. Set crystal clear intentions every day and use them to charge you up and move you toward what turns you on. You can utilize your sensuality and body wisdom to find your flow again when you might feel otherwise apathetic or stuck.

 GUARDIAN—Earth beings show up for the people they care about with a listening ear and stay grounded no matter what life throws at them. You, earthly one, are a lover through and through, and it shows up in how you treat the people you care about. Your devotion for life is also activated when you connect with nature. There is something sensual about connecting to the land, feeling the dirt on your toes and leaves touching your skin, isn't there? Intentionally make space for you to play, have fun, and revel in the juiciness of simply being alive. These moments will help you remember your passion and what it is that's truly important to you.

CHAPTER SIX

Ethos

Own Your Voice to Live Your Truth

ETHOS (noun): The characteristic spirit of a culture, era, or community as manifested in its beliefs and aspirations.

Like most of us, I grew up in a world that told me rebellion is a punishable offense. I learned that in order to survive, it was important for me to blend in and be like everyone else. But when I looked around, I realized that most of the adults in my life seemed both unhappy and unfulfilled. They didn't express their creativity, nor did they ponder life beyond that well-worn path of "shoulds" and "musts." Something about it felt superficial. I was supposed to want the same things—fancy cars, a giant mansion, designer brands, following the latest trends, and fitting into what was popular—but I didn't. And I just couldn't bring myself to fake it. And even when I tried, it was obvious that I wasn't being real. Because those things weren't actually aligned with what was important to me.

To cope with this conflict growing up, I disengaged with life. I got D's and F's in school and stayed out late trying to understand what made me feel alive. Eventually, as I got older, I realized that wasn't quite working so I tried another approach. I wanted to get out of Las Vegas and didn't know another way than to play the game the way others expected. I started applying myself and getting amazing grades in college. For the first time, I was a straight A student. I felt validated, but I still wanted something more. The negative messages I'd received about the risks of pursuing my creativity wore heavy on my soul. I didn't know any other entrepreneurs. There were no clear examples of queer artists of color I could look to for inspiration (or at least I didn't know where to find them). So I followed a conventional path of academia that appeased my parents because I didn't really know I had any other options. My happy medium was studying art and artists, but a lot of people condescendingly asked me what I expected to do with that degree, assuming that I had wasted money and time studying something useless.

Defend the Sacred

When I had just graduated college, I was only willing to work in a creative field. But my options were severely limited. At first, I decided to pursue museum work since my undergraduate degree was in art history. I wanted to share my knowledge, love, and passion for the arts with museum visitors. However, museum jobs were notorious for overworking and underpaying employees. The competition was stiff, and almost every art history grad was willing to work for free because the field was so competitive. Having no experience further limited my chances of being selected for a paid position. Thinking museums would be the organization that shared my beliefs and priorities, I begged and prayed for an opportunity to prove my worth and get my foot in the door. I knew I was applying for the lowest paid positions with very little opportunity for a salary increase, but that didn't stop me from trying to prove myself and be seen.

When I googled "what to wear for a job interview," I found a set of photos of women in knee-length skirts and solid-colored button-up shirts. The looks were practical. Expected. Traditional. Modest heels, which I never wear, were encouraged. So I put my discomfort aside, because getting the job seemed paramount. However, even though I looked the part and had the degree, I still didn't get any of the jobs.

Each rejection sent me further into a downward spiral of striving to be seen. If I tried with everything I had within me to be accepted and validated, but still didn't fit in, what did that say about me? These rejections steadily chipped away any sliver of hope that I might one day share my gifts with the world and get paid for it. For millennials like me, the promise of the American Dream is perforated with uncertainty. Many of my peers are struggling under massive student loan debt, getting crushed in underpaid jobs, and working around the clock with little hope of ever purchasing their own home and finding financial stability, let alone freedom. Terrified about my future, I abandoned my dreams in the hopes that someone else would come along and rescue me in the form of a job offer in a creative field. To tell me that I am worthy of getting paid to do what I love, am good at, and am passionate about.

For so many years, I was gripped with worry about other people's perceptions of me. Do they like me? Will they accept me? Who do I need to be in order to be worthy in their eyes? Can they tell I'm queer? Am I South Asian enough? Am I cool enough? Did I say the right thing? Did I wear the right thing? I doubted myself constantly.

I realize now that what I was seeking could only be found within me. The approval and validation that I needed was my own. And no one else could give it to me. The missing piece that kept me from standing confidently in my ability to make a difference was my need to sit with myself and honor my truth. Instead of asking what everyone else wanted of me, I needed to affirm what I desired. I needed to be with my own emotions and honor them. I needed to discover what moves me, what I believe in, and why. But I was so concerned with what everyone else was doing and what I thought they wanted me to be that I never gave myself the time or space to understand my own ethos—the values that drive my life. So I pulled out my journal, got still and quiet, and did the following exercise.

❥⤜⤜⟫⟫ CREATIVE PRACTICE ⟪⟪⤛⤛❥
Journal Assignment

This exercise will help you understand your authentic values. It's something I learned from **anti-racist** business educator Trudi Lebron.[1] Anti-racism is the practice of creating policies, practices, ideologies, and worldviews that eliminate racism at the individual and structural level. As Trudi states, the goal of antiracism is equity and diversity. That means that it's up to each of us to do the inner work required to **decolonize your mind** so that we can create a world in which everyone is invited to the party and has access to the opportunities you bring through your Creative Mission.

No matter what identities you carry, it's important that you look at the ways in which you may have internalized the racist, homophobic, or transphobic messaging that our society is steeped with. If you carry marginalized identities, it's likely that you may have internalized some of this oppression. For me, that meant that for a long time, I was afraid to speak up for what I believed in. But your silence on important social issues is not helping anyone. In fact, if more people spoke up on behalf of others with less privilege, we could probably reimagine the world a lot faster to be a safer and more inclusive space for Wildhearts of all walks of life. And that is *so important.*

Being connected to your values will put you on the path toward creating a life that's truly in alignment for you, one that you feel proud of and that you know is beneficial to more people than just yourself. This will increase your confidence because you will know that every action you take is standing for something you believe in and an important part of the bigger change that you hope to see happen on the planet. So often we don't pause to consider what our values are. And the things we think we believe are actually the values of others or the dominant cultural narrative that we've taken on as our own without stopping to examine where these beliefs came from.

This exercise will help you get clear on your own values versus those that you think you are *supposed to* believe in. I want you to move throughout the world embodying exactly what you stand for and knowing your unique *why* behind it. Why do these issues matter to you? Once you know what your values are, you can use them to guide your decisions and help bring you closer to your Creative Mission.

PART 1: Set a timer for five minutes. During that time, write a list of every value you can think of. Go fast and don't think too hard. Just get as many values down as you can for the full five minutes.

PART 2: Take another five minutes to organize your values into no more than five broad categories. You'll notice that many of your values can be clustered together as subcategories of one another. Title your categories in ways that resonate with you. Use words that feel meaningful to you. For example, some keywords for your categories might include creativity, representation, anti-racism, inclusivity, simplicity, mindfulness, or community.

THE OUTER INVITATION TO FIND MY TRUE INNER SELF

When I arrived on campus at Smith College after spending two years at a community college, I wanted to put my all into studying creativity. I chose Smith because it seemed perfect for a 20-year-old who was just barely coming to terms with her sexuality as a queer person. Smith is a wildly radical school with a rebellious history, educating classic Wildhearts like Julia Child and Sylvia Plath. On top of that, the school has a very progressive culture with regard to gender, sexuality, women's studies, and is more open to conversations about decolonizing academia in general. The vast majority of the student body identified as LGBTQ+. In addition, it was as far away from Las Vegas as I could get and a safe haven where I could come out to myself, while also getting an objectively amazing education so I could learn a ton about art and art history at a prestigious school with a fabulous art department. Smith even had its own museum of art, where I worked many roles, from being an art conservator in the basement laboratory to making coffee in the atrium café. It was the perfect place for me.

While it was a great fit, it took me a while to get comfortable there. Everyone around me seemed out and proud. They were connected to their values and spoke up for their beliefs. They seemed comfortable in their own skin. They were edgy and authentic and unafraid to stand up for what they believed in. I wanted to express myself with the same passion and confidence as my peers did. Yet there I was, just barely coming to terms with my own identity for the first time.

I had lived most of my life without exploring many parts of myself that had existed since I was a young teenager, and probably even before that. I hadn't yet examined what it meant to be a femme of color; a South Asian; a first-generation American; a queer Muslim; an artist, along with so many other intersecting identities. I didn't feel like I knew who I was and was afraid to talk about what I stood for out of fear that I didn't know enough or would somehow "get it wrong." And this left me with those familiar awkward, anxious feelings of not being confident, and disembodied in my truth. It was disheartening, and it would have been so much easier to just say, "Why bother?"

The first time I had a cute girl in my dorm room, we were connecting, just getting to know each other as friends and talking about our experiences on a new campus. I definitely had a mild crush on her and was excited to make a new friend on campus. So I did what everyone does when they flirt. I spontaneously burst into tears. This was embarrassing because I used to be so uncomfortable crying or showing vulnerability in front of others, let alone crush-worthy girls. Thankfully, she was super sweet about it. In a tearful confession, I blurted out, "I just don't understand how you're so comfortable with yourself. Everyone here is so confident being queer, and I'm just . . . not." Then she told me that there were parts of her queerness and identity that she too was just starting to understand. She shared a story about an encounter she had with a transwoman at the café. They had a beautiful conversation that helped her realize how much she still had to learn about the trans experience. In that moment, I felt a little more normalized and understood that it was okay to still be in my own process of discovering myself.

I grew up experiencing a lot of shame around the truth of who I am. Outside influences made me feel like there was something wrong with me because I was "different." I was creative. I was queer. I was anything but traditional. Now I recognize these are feelings that almost every queer person faces. I looked to everyone else for answers on how to belong and fit in. I found myself smitten with other creatives and their work. Whether it was a song, performance, or article, their words and values awakened something inside of me that I longed to embrace and express outwardly. Now I realize my attraction to these people was based on the way they embodied their values and expressed themselves so authentically in the world. Because I needed that too to feel truly comfortable in my own skin.

There was so much inside of me that wanted to be expressed. But I didn't feel confident enough to unleash it. In fact, I didn't feel worthy enough to even explore it. Instead, I filled my plate with activities and accomplishments, trying to find that sense of validation. To be chosen. But it was never enough. I was missing my own sense of values—an ethos I could embody that would bolster me past those Inner Overprotectors that held me back and tried to keep me safe. I got the message from other Wildhearts at Smith that it was powerful to be honest about who you are. It inspired me. The fact that you can be different, revolutionary, and subversive while still being smart, accomplished, and empowered. It spoke to something inside of me that I didn't yet have the courage to express. In all of my seeking, I needed to carve out the actual time and space to explore who I was and what I believed in order to really embody my values.

Eventually I went on to build a six-figure business, teaching marketing and business without ever naming that I, myself, am a queer woman of color and that my identities and experiences growing up inextricably shaped my perspective of the world. I was afraid of what might happen if I truly came out of the closet. Even worse, I shunned the creativity conversation altogether because I wasn't sure if anyone would pay money to learn about creativity from me, since I internalized the belief that creativity isn't a valuable or worthy pursuit. Along my journey of trying to get paid and survive, I abandoned parts of myself that were inherent to my wholeness. After a few years, I realized I was attracting the wrong type of clients for my business.

At one of my annual year-end retreats, I was surprised to see that every single person who attended fit into the same category that didn't reflect any of my own identities or values. They were mostly young, white, "spiritual," or new-age types who really didn't care about social justice values or equity. Many of them had approached me with an entitled energy that didn't feel good. I felt like I had to perform and constantly say yes in order to keep them happy. Yet I felt I had no right to say anything about it because they had invested money in my services. And if they paid me, I must owe them everything, right? So I bent over backward, trying to keep everyone happy. I answered messages outside of working hours and ran myself ragged trying to be everything they wanted me to be. This was me acting out of alignment with my own ethos. In reality, standing stronger in the fact that I was a queer woman of color making a name for myself would have helped me construct my own version of spirituality and business: one that does not center whiteness and one that honors my humanity. This wildly creative act of reclaiming my own identity was my responsibility and a part of my Creative Mission, so that I could pave the way for others who saw themselves in my authentic story, not the fabricated one that I thought would be more palatable for the world.

For a long time, I put on the facade of being a liberated artist. But there were still many ways in which I was holding myself back, not honoring myself, and not speaking up for the issues that mattered to me. It wasn't until I started writing this book that I had a very painful realization. It became obvious that I, myself, hadn't been centering the people that I wanted to speak to, the people who moved through the world with experiences similar to mine. In tears, I asked my mentor, "How do I speak to other queer women of color?" I was in agony at the realization that I didn't know how to speak to myself. I had been abandoning and ignoring myself and, in the process, lots of other people like me who deserved to be heard. I had been conditioned to center whiteness, and as a result, I had put myself on the margins in my own life.

My healing journey began when I put my ethos at the forefront. Now I know that my creativity is a vehicle through which I can heal myself, and when I do, it's healing for other people too. The results of taking action in alignment with my own ethos have been so liberating. I'm proud to say my business coaching programs are among the most diverse in the industry. At the time of writing this, 70 percent of my students identify as people of color, 50 percent identify as LGBTQ+, and 40 percent identify as queer people of color.

I also receive messages on a regular basis from others who have heard my story and decided to come out of the closet in their own lives. I never expected that by stepping into my Creative Mission, I would be able to be the role model that I always needed when I was younger. But now, this has become one of my biggest motivators.

This shift in my programs is a direct result of the personal work I've done to lead with my values and infuse them into every aspect of my life through my Creative Mission. And it trickles out into my business and the lives of the people I serve. My clients go on to help their clients find more truth and freedom in their lives. And it moves them as much as it moves me. My Creative Mission has attracted the right type of people in my life. Those who are a fit for who I truly am. I don't have to hide anymore or pretend to be someone I'm not. I can be me, I can speak my truth, and I now know that doing so will create an environment in which I can expand, rather than contract.

Expansion Exercise

EMBODY YOUR VALUES

Now that you're clear about what some of your values are, I want you to assess whether you are embodying these values in all areas in your life. When you embody your values and live them, you'll notice more abundance coming your way. You will walk with more confidence knowing that you're in alignment with what's important to you, and you'll be less likely to self-sabotage and get in your own way when you know that your actions are in alignment with the change that you want to see in the world. Grab your Abudance Journal and answer the following questions.

- ✦ What five values are most important to you? Revisit your answers in the previous exercise in this chapter and list them here again.

- ✦ How are you embodying these values in the following areas:
    - ★ Your creativity
    - ★ Your purpose
    - ★ Your relationships
    - ★ Your sense of self-love

- ✦ How can you start embodying your values more in each of these areas?

Bonus art assignment

Make a piece of art with your five values and hang your artwork near your creative space or workspace. Keep revisiting these values and use them as a guide for your decision-making from this point forward. If you ever wonder what your next step should be, ask yourself which option is most in alignment with these values and decide from there.

Teaching

TRUST YOURSELF AND
YOUR CREATIVE IMPULSE

Growing up in Las Vegas, I saw how toxic our capitalist culture can be. I saw the objectification of women and how we toss aside anything that doesn't seem new or sparkly. To me, it was obvious that corporations capitalized on our insecurities, big-time. If you're unhappy with how you look or are always chasing after the latest trends, chances are you're going to spend more money. The good news is that businesses are beginning to change. With the direction the world is going in, we want companies that lead with their values. You'll notice that many of the latest marketing trends show the ways that companies are giving back to meaningful causes. Happiness is fleeting, but living a life of purpose is something that no one can ever take away from you.

As younger generations of the world grow up, they are demanding that organizations have a strong ethos in order to be competitive in the marketplace. For me, I will always much rather invest in companies that have values that align with mine. If you don't know what your values are, and you just try to do what has always been done in the past, you are missing out on a huge opportunity to shine in your ethos. And you may be replicating systems that are not in service to the evolution of our world into a place that's more inclusive, creative, and healing for all. Furthermore, if you do what everyone else does, you'll just blend into the crowd. Lead with your ethos and you will not only find your people, but you will also find the people who support you and want to invest in your Creative Mission. And you'll stand out in the best way, by being exactly who you are without trying so hard to be anyone else.

Just Be Yourself

The key to being a confident creative is to become deeply connected to your own personal ethos. Often people say, "Just be yourself." But learning how to be yourself is clearly much easier said than done. If it were that simple, we would all be Radiant Wildhearts blazing a trail toward our Creative Mission without fear.

There are many reasons why it's easier to follow the crowd than it is to blaze your own path. You might be afraid of what others will think of you if you ruffle some feathers by disagreeing with them. You might not be clear what your values even are because you haven't taken the time to check in and see what you believe or how your ethos is evolving over time.

Many people choose to follow the path well-traveled because it seems safe. But here's the problem with taking the safe path: it's overcrowded. It takes a lot of courage and bravery to stand in the things that make you unique, particularly if they were sources of pain, criticism, or ridicule when you were younger. Being a Radiant Wildheart means embracing all the parts of yourself that you felt did not belong. As you unpack that which makes you feel like a misfit, you will find your own personal ethos that will guide you for the rest of your journey.

In order to build your own ethos, you'll probably have to break with tradition. That means being innovative and trusting your creative impulses. To be able to do that, you get to face your fears and speak up when it matters to you. Trust me when I say that life gets so much easier when you let yourself stand in your truth instead of trying to fight or hide it. The sooner you let yourself relax into simply being you, the easier your journey toward total creative self-expression will be.

INNER OVERPROTECTOR

The Chameleon

When it comes to living by your ethos, one type of Inner Overprotector may be holding you back: the Chameleon. The Chameleon means no harm. It wants you to fit in and be popular, but they're afraid of what might happen if people find out you are wildly unique and different. The Chameleon protects a wound that probably goes back generations for you and your family.

Historically, those who were different were often punished. For example, women who were single, queer, and/or psychic were burned at the stake instead of revered for their ability to heal. The Chameleon's job is to blend in, change colors, and adapt to its environment as a means of protection. When the Chameleon is running the show, you'll feel insecure about your own creative impulses. You'll look externally for ideas of how you should look, dress, or be in order to blend into your surroundings. You'll become stuck in an observer role, rather than fully embodying your unique creative magic.

When you are firm in your values, however, you will be more solid in yourself. Then you won't feel as much of a need to morph into other people.

Here are signs that you're ruled by the Chameleon:

✦ You're trying to impress everyone around you.

✦ You're constantly trying to emulate other people.

✦ You don't have a clear sense of your values and change them based on who you're with.

✦ You feel like a different person based on who you are hanging out with.

✦ You're focused on the latest trends but don't know what you actually like.

✦ You don't think your opinions are as intelligent, witty, or cool as those of other people in your life, so you don't share them.

Tips for dealing with the Chameleon: Spend time with your personal practices and creative practices. When you spend time with yourself, your truth starts to emerge and even becomes impossible to ignore. Find ways to explore your own creativity, even if that means enrolling yourself in a creative class to hold you accountable to showing up for your creativity. Your practices are where you get to know your true self.

If you are consistently looking outside of yourself for validation, make a ritual out of releasing that tendency and stepping into a new way of being. One where you choose to intentionally validate and acknowledge yourself for all the beauty and magic you bring to the world. Remember, seeking validation and approval outside of yourself is only a temporary fix. The real medicine is when you can source that from within. Showing up for your personal practices is a great way to build the muscle of recognizing what your truth is and making decisions accordingly.

Archetype Spotlight

CREATE A LIFE AROUND YOUR VALUES

 MYSTIC—Because you are ethereal and connected to your divine knowing, Mystics might have a difficult time identifying the values that are really important to themselves here on planet Earth. You might have a natural tendency toward **spiritual bypassing**, which, honestly, mystical one, isn't a good look in this lifetime. Spiritual bypassing is when you hide behind spirituality in a way that prevents you from facing unresolved emotional issues or collective social issues. When you are spiritually bypassing, you might ignore the truth because it doesn't feel "high vibe" enough. However, our world holds both divinity and the shadows. Your own spiritual journey is going to be a mixed bag of positive emotions and difficult ones. Can you allow yourself to really feel it all, even those things that may not be comfortable to look at? You can really amplify your power if you connect to causes that are bigger than yourself here on this planet. Spend time identifying your values and putting them into words that resonate with you so that you can serve on a deeper level.

 VISIONARY—Air beings constantly think about the collective and the future vision that they see for their community. You are looking for ways to evolve, and that Visionary nature of yours is magnified by your ability to be guided by your values and an ethos uniquely your own. This is one of your strengths, so lean into it because it will make your Creative Mission so much more magnetic.

SACRED REBEL—Fire beings are driven by their passions and fueled by the inner drive and motivation to create transformation in this lifetime. By connecting to your ethos, you will always know that you are on a path that is deeply meaningful for you and serving a higher purpose by helping others too. Connect with your values to make sure that you're staying in integrity. Don't burn any bridges by taking a "by any means necessary" approach.

 HEALER—Water beings are connected to an inner emotional reality that can provide an excellent compass identifying core values. If something is keeping you up at night or has you feeling bothered, you might need to come into more alignment with one of your values. Seek out environments where you feel safe to express yourself, your values, and your boundaries. Make sure that you aren't bending over backward for others or people pleasing in a way that doesn't honor your ethos and self-worth.

 GUARDIAN—Earth beings have a natural value of staying in integrity with their ethos. You want to do things in an ethical way that feels aligned for you, and sometimes you won't take any action until you feel that everything has clicked into alignment. You care about what's important like protecting the planet and other beings on it, so you naturally lead with your values.

PART III

Liberate Yourself through Wild Self-Expression

Now that you've reestablished your relationship to your inner artist, it's time to break through those layers of conditioning and liberate yourself to express the real you in the world outside of what the world and society has told you to be. This is your full-spectrum self. Your inner artist that has integrated all of the parts that make you unique and different. From there, you can use all of those parts like colors on palette to create your life however you want it to be.

This reclamation will happen through your creative practice. And no matter what your creative practice is, it requires devotion. It requires a recommitment to showing up even when it feels scary or uncomfortable, even when your to-do list is miles long and filled with things that seem more "important." The more devoted you are to your practices, the easier it will be to live your truth without second-guessing yourself. This is imperative for your liberation and embodiment of your most badass, fully expressed self.

Don't worry if you've struggled to be consistent with your creativity in the past. I'll help you uncover how to embrace your free-spirited nature and express it through your artistry so that you can finally liberate your Radiant Wildheart from any boxes that have you feeling confined. First, you will get into a flow state that will help you access your truth with ease and presence as you create. From there, you'll do an ecstatic deep dive into pleasure. I'll show you how to weave yummy bliss into every area of your life, especially your creative practices so it feels amazing to show up for yourself in this way. Finally, you'll learn how to heal through wild self-expression, unafraid to live your truth and share it with the world. And as an added bonus, when you create with the intention of healing yourself, you'll understand how to help others and make a difference in the world just by being yourself.

So, Wildheart, I invite you to dive deep into this section and give yourself the gift of your full presence. Play full-out with the creative embodiment practices and stretch into new places you might not have been before. Give yourself permission to revel in all of the juicy feelings that come up, and push yourself through the challenging parts of this process. I promise, what's on the other side is something you've been desiring for lifetimes. Remember, you're here to be liberated by any means necessary, so let your mind take the passenger seat and invite your Intuitive Higher Self to take the wheel. It's time to liberate your Radiant Wildheart by accessing all of the revolutionary joy, pleasure, and healing that wants to flow through you now.

I wish you so many blessings in this sacred moment of your journey. I know for me, cultivating a consistent creative practice has been one of the greatest struggles in my life. I hope with the teachings that follow, you'll find the ease and fun of tending to your inner artist on a consistent basis and letting your Radiant Wildheart come out to play.

CHAPTER SEVEN

Creativity

Show Up for Your Revolution!

For many years, I accessed my creativity by facilitating creative experiences for others. Whether it was in the classroom or in a community with my nonprofit, I found a way to turn my creativity into work, because I believed it was all that I wanted to do. But even though I was being creative for a living and had relatively stable employment as an art educator, I deeply longed for my own personal creative practice. I wanted to feel fully expressed, and I still didn't.

I invested in all the tools and had an entire closet dedicated to acrylic paints, charcoal, colored pencils, watercolor, jewelry-making supplies, a sewing kit, scrapbooking supplies, henna tools, and lots of musical instruments. But most of them sat untouched in the dark for years, collecting dust.

I had struggled with emotional challenges and mindset blocks for my entire life, and I intuitively knew that my creativity would be the gateway to my healing. I wanted to feel confident and embodied as an artist. Like I was making my mark and creating a body of work that expressed what I felt inside. I spent tons of money on coaching sessions, trying to figure how I could finally make the space for my own creativity. I told everyone that I wanted to paint more, I wanted to play music, I wanted to dance. But no matter how much I claimed it, it never seemed to happen.

Every time I sat down to write, paint, or make music, I would feel a familiar tightening in my throat. Those Inner Overprotectors would start to go off, telling me that I was an inadequate artist. I would tap into intense feelings, emotions, memories, and a void that I didn't even know was in there. These were the things that I tried to numb myself from. And it was a lot easier to run, to build a life that was way too busy to find time to make art. Eventually, however, I couldn't run away any longer. I had to find it within myself to sit down and consistently create in a way that was both liberating and accessible. I had to tackle my own resistance and fears in order to finally be free. And to do that, I had to create for me, not for anyone else.

Of course, being the Sacred Rebel that I am, I had to do it in my own way. I had to focus on how I felt when I was in the act of creation, rather than put the emphasis on how good the final product was. I had to enjoy the process instead of constantly thinking about the end goal. It took devotion and practice before I was able to break through all of these internal judgments and stop editing myself as I created.

Now when I paint, I am totally unattached to what the finished outcome looks like. I trust my intuition and know that nothing on the canvas is permanent and everything could change in a moment. When I dance, I prefer to flow with the music rather than learn choreography and steps that I have to memorize. When I learn a new instrument, I spend time feeling it on my fingers and getting curious about what sounds I can make before I learn all of the scales that preface most music theory books. I let myself create in the moment, without any sort of planning, because that's what feels pleasurable in my body. Because this allows me to get out of my head and into the present moment, which ultimately is the medicine that I and so many others need.

I realized that I was stalled in my own artistic growth because I didn't take the time to practice the art of getting out of my head and into the present moment. Because that's where the real magic happens. And I didn't take the time to practice painting or music, just like I resisted my meditation and yoga practice. Because showing up is half the battle. And I hadn't found a way to make it fun yet.

Instead, I was so hard on myself for not being initially "good" at what-ever medium I was working with. Like a lot of us do, I sucked all the fun out of it. For example, I got my first guitar at age nine, but I didn't prac-tice enough to embody some chords with fluidity until I was 30. And I entertained the idea of writing this book for about two years before I actually put pen to paper and started fleshing out these pages. I had to learn to stop editing myself and let my thoughts and feelings spill out into the world. And now I want to learn how to produce my first music album, and I'm working on letting music flow from within me—from that cre-ative spirit that I can feel and want to fully embody and express, without overthinking it.

I know now that showing up to your creative practice isn't necessarily about learning the "rules" and the "how-to" as much as it is about being comfortable with yourself. To allow yourself to find that flow state and enjoy the ride. This is true for every medium. If you can get out of your thoughts and immerse yourself in the feeling of creation, magic happens and masterpieces are channeled without even trying.

I still struggle with finding that consistency. I find my groove but then step out of the beat, and that's okay. Maybe it's because I find myself getting too busy. Or maybe I get so wrapped up in one project that I forget about the other mediums that call to me. Or maybe it's because living in that flow state, being present, and feeling everything can be intense. It's natural to have some resistance to conjuring up all of the emotions that live inside of you. Especially the ones that you've tried to suppress for so long. Your truth might even shock you at first. And that's an exhilarating place to be.

When I started to embody my inner artist, I realized I needed to make it a point to show up for my creativity even when I didn't feel like it. Because underneath that resistance, something sacred was waiting to be revealed to me. And that's where the devotional aspect of your creativity comes in handy. Over time, the more I remembered *why* I want to show up for this, and everything that's on the other side, the more I can stop judging myself and let myself play. And the more fun you're having, the more you will love what you create.

Now I have no qualms about sitting my friends down, plugging my microphone into a giant speaker, and singing them a half-finished breakup song with my whole heart. And even if my singing isn't pitch-perfect, they'll love it as much as I do because they'll feel my authenticity. And that is the gift that keeps on giving. When I paint, I throw colors at the canvas and I don't care what it looks like. Then I listen. To what wants to happen next, to how my body wants to move, and to what marks want to intuitively come out of me. I'll analyze it later. When I'm starting a song, I'll freestyle to a beat, loving the fact that no one will ever hear what I say but me. If I can get out of my own critical mind, It's total freedom, and it feels so fun.

All of my masterpieces are born from giving myself permission to play and letting myself be moved rather than trying to force things. Emancipating myself from anyone else's judgements. My art is for me.

I'm finally happy to say that I create art all the time. Not just visual art, but music, dance, and writing. And not just traditional arts, but I live my life as a wild act of self-expression. It's in everything I touch. From the clothes that I wear, to how I spend my time, and how I structure my relationships. Creativity is a state of mind and a way of being for me. But it requires a constant recommitment to showing up for what's important to me, and to listening to how things want to evolve. The more I do, the more my creativity flows, taking me to vibrant and colorful places that I never could have anticipated. And that's what's so exciting about it.

My creative practice is about listening. Listening to my Intuitive Higher Self, to my inner child, to my truth. Through my art, I explore myself and understand what life is teaching me. I integrate who I am with what I know. I embrace aspects of myself that I used to think made me a terrible artist, like my inability to stay inside of the lines or to not drip paint everywhere. Now those things have become a part of my style. Messy. Colorful. Wild and free. It's my essence. That which sets me apart and makes my work unique. I've always longed for attention and approval. Now I give that to myself through my creative practices, letting myself become the artist that I've always admired.

The art that brings me closer to myself is the art that feels liberating to make. The more I trust my creative flow, the more of myself is revealed to me. And then I can share that with the world though my Creative Mission. And it resonates with others, because it's so deeply aligned to who I am that it's undeniable. And it activates something in the people who get to experience it. My resilience is felt and I know that my art moves people to find more of themselves too. And no one will ever be able to take that away from me.

My creativity is a way of life. It shows up everywhere, and I refuse to restrict it to any one particular medium because I know that everything I touch can become art. My need to express myself fully in the world is insatiable. I believe that we all long to be seen as our authentic selves. Our inner children are all artists wanting to be set free! I lived my life hiding for so long that now it's undeniable how healing it is to be seen in my truth, no matter how scary it might feel in the moment. When I get out of my head and into my heart, my creativity flows. And I want us all to feel liberated enough to express the beauty that we bring to the world through our art.

WHAT IS FLOW?

In order to access your wild creativity, you need to understand the importance of flow in your life. So many of us have been taught that our time is only well spent if we are doing something "productive." As a culture, we tend to prioritize the analytical, logical, and practical left-brain activities without acknowledging that even disciplines like math and science encompass so much creativity! Our evolution and growth is a result of getting curious, asking the right questions, and trusting intuitive nudges that guide us forward. Whether you're painting or dancing or completing a science experiment or baking a cake, there are endless opportunities to make creative choices in your life.

In your creative practice, tapping into flow space will help you remember your ability to experiment and play, which will keep your creativity moving forward without getting stuck in overthinking land. Flow space is the state of mind in which you can be fully present and focused on the activities you're doing. Others call this a flow state, but I like flow space better because the point of being in flow is to create lots of space within for your true expression to emerge. There are many different types of flow spaces and just as many ways to tap into them. When you are in a flow space, you are truly living in the moment. You are leading with the wisdom of your Intuitive Higher Self, without letting your anxiety or Inner Overprotectors dictate your actions or choices. This doesn't necessarily mean that you won't have any intrusive thoughts, but just like we do in meditation, you can simply acknowledge them and then allow yourself to keep flowing. I've found that the more time and space I give myself to enter into a flow state, the more effective I am in all other areas of my life and the clearer my own creative channel becomes.

In college I took an incredible class called "The Meaning of Life." It was an intro to philosophy course that required us to read various texts from different religions and philosophers offering their interpretation of how to make life meaningful. I will never forget what I learned about flow from the Daoist texts that we read. Daoism says that we often focus on the shape and form of our world and create meaning from there. But actually, it's the space in between that makes anything useful. Take, for example, a bowl. When you think of a bowl, you probably think of the object itself: a concave piece of dishware that you probably have stacks of in your kitchen cupboard. But what makes the bowl useful is the space in between the form. What makes it valuable is actually what's not there— that hollowed-out center that allows you to hold your food or whatever else you need to store within it.

The same is true for your own creativity. Without carving out some time and space for you to have flow in your life, you can't access your full potential. If you are always busy doing, when will you have time to just be with the creativity that wants to move through you? In the sacred creativity temple you are building out of your life, you will need a balance of structure and flow.

When I work with magical Radiant Wildhearts who are highly creative, they're sometimes resistant to adding more structure into their lives. But what I've found is that structure can help you create more freedom in your life. Structure is the way you set yourself up to have access to creative flow states on a regular, consistent basis. For example, by putting time into your calendar that you leave open and unscheduled to flow and do whatever you feel like. This empty space can be hugely inspiring and where your best ideas will flow from.

So let flow seduce you. Let yourself slow down and dance with life by creating space for you to move in any direction that your Intuitive Higher Self wants to go. No walls or ceilings, just lots of expansive space to hold all of your creative brilliance.

Teaching

TAPPING INTO FLOW

I've spoken to so many people who feel the deep longing for their creativity the way that I always have. Like, without it, something important is missing. If you're feeling that too, just remember that longing is there for a reason. You might not know exactly what your creativity wants to bring into your life, but the reason you're reading this book is because part of you is ready to be liberated and wildly self-expressed. Society might have tricked you into thinking your creativity isn't valuable and what you want to share isn't important. But that's far from the truth. Your creativity holds the key to your freedom. That's why you are here, showing up for it, even if it's not exactly a comfortable or easy process.

It's hard to fathom the impact creativity has on our lives. Everything that you love comes from someone saying yes to their creativity. Think about it: if we didn't have creativity, society as we know it wouldn't exist. All of the art, movies, music, engineering feats, and tech inventions that you love and use every day all came from someone thinking creatively to solve the problems they saw in the world. Look around you. Everything you see started as an idea or a question taken to its end. Creativity makes us human. It's infinite. Life would be mundane and colorless without creativity. Research totally backs this up. For example, schools with arts education programs have better attendance in all classes.[1] And when we bring creativity into all aspects of life, we're more effective, present, and alive in all of the roles we play.

How can you make it easier to access your creativity throughout the day? Look for signs and messages that inspire you. Entertain those random thoughts that pop into your mind. They're messages directly from your inner muses. I recommend keeping either a notebook or a notes app on your phone so you can write down these inspired messages as you receive them. Later, pull from your notes to inspire you in whatever you're working on. Let your creativity influence the way you perceive the world, and eventually you'll be in flow with your Creative Mission.

Infinite Creativity

We live in an abundant universe. Similarly, our creativity is limitless. Your creative mind is running all of the time, even when you don't realize it. Heck, even when we sleep, we are dreaming up imaginary worlds. While you might "should" yourself for not doing enough, our inner artists are always creating and teaching us new things. As my creativity mentor, SARK says, any time we can tap into the creative flow that's always happening beneath the surface of our rational minds, it's wisdom.

Even if you don't feel like you have been tapping into your creativity on a regular basis, you are making creative choices every day. The way you dress yourself, the food you make, how you parent your kids or nurture the people in your life—all of this is creative. The more time you spend in your creative practice, the more you will strengthen your relationship to that creative voice and your inner artist so that you feel more confident as you explore your self-expression.

One of my favorite tricks is to make things up as I go. The reality is that most of us have no idea what we are doing. Some of my best ideas have come from just making things up on the spot. I often surprise myself with how much I actually know. On many occasions, I've created something out of thin air, simply by declaring it to be so. When I first started mentoring people to grow their businesses, I didn't have a ton of business experience. My ability to tie my experiences in business and project management with my background in creativity was pretty spontaneous. It was born through a process of repeatedly saying yes to the messages that were channeling through me directly from my inner muses.

Give yourself permission to trust your intuitive voice and let it guide you into unexpected places. It's from those places that your most prolific creative ideas will be found.

Words cast spells. The things you say dictate your mindset and your actions. For example, one of my biggest beliefs around business is that the more fun you're having, the more money you'll make. I didn't have a lot of evidence to back up this claim, but I wanted it to be true. So I declared it to be so. When I started to approach my business as though this were true, the universe affirmed to me that I was onto something.

The more I declare something to be real, the more my subconscious mind gets on board, and the faster it manifests into reality. Anyone who studies the law of attraction will tell you the same thing. The power of speaking affirmations and reprogramming the subconscious will help you reach your goals. What if, instead of giving so much energy to our fear, we put that energy into declaring and writing the world as we want to see it. The more you write it and change the script in your mind, eventually your actions will align. It's inevitable. What if we invest our energy into being solution-focused and creative rather than stopping at the usual places we get stuck. Making it up as you go helps you develop trust that you can handle whatever life brings your way and that every misstep is an opportunity for more growth and refinement.

Stop Judging Yourself

The only way to get into flow with your creativity is to stop judging yourself and your creations while you are in the process of creating. There are a million reasons we are constantly judging and critiquing ourselves as we create. For me, I have a pattern of thinking about what everyone else might think of my creativity as I'm creating it. This is the fastest way I kick myself out of the flow.

It's natural to want to create things that you and others like. You probably have an idea in your mind about your art and how you want it to look. For beginners, your skills might not be in a place where the art you make looks the way you expected it to in your mind. But even then, there's magic in your mistakes and, as painting teacher extraordinaire Bob Ross says, in the "happy accidents" that occur when you let flow lead the way.

It's okay if things don't come out as planned. You can always build upon the surprises that happen when you're leading with your Intuitive Higher Self. Think about it. All of your favorite artists probably spent months or years refining their craft before they presented the work that inspired you. When you see a finished product, you are only seeing the tip of the iceberg. Remember that comparison is a true creativity killer.

When you find that you're comparing yourself to people who are farther down the road in their own creative practices, remember that you have no idea about the creative process it took to get to the final result. The point of your creative practices is to strengthen the muscle of listening to your Visionary voice. The more you listen, the more you'll be able to let yourself just show up authentically, as you are, without the extra baggage of trying to be what you think other people want.

Flow Space and Be Time

Here are some quick ways to tap into flow space:

- Focus on your breathing or do a breathwork exercise.
- Meditate or do a moving meditation for five minutes.
- Turn your phone off and be fully present on the task at hand.
- Make a gratitude list to help you focus on what's really important to you.
- Make your breakfast with deep intentional presence.

The more I practice being in flow, the easier it becomes. Below is a noncomprehensive list of some of the flow spaces I like to enter. But remember, there is no right or wrong way to be in a flow space. You get to define what flow space means to you and what you need from it at any given moment.

Freestyling

When you freestyle, you let yourself express whatever comes to mind without overthinking it. Freestyling can take such forms as speaking, singing, writing, or dancing. It can also look like creating a yummy meal based solely on your intuition. Or choosing to take a walk with no planned destination. This is the space where you let yourself play and explore. The only rule is that it needs to be totally unplanned. This is a lot easier said than done. When I first started freestyling, especially in front of other people, I found myself face-to-face with my own fears. Freestyling is about allowing yourself to say your ideas out loud. Bring your words, your poem, your song, your creative self forward and let it flow! Even if it comes out a little messy, who cares? The point is to access the magical moments that occur when you give your inner-artist permission to be spontaneous and free.

Ecstatic Dance

I'm writing this from my current home, close to the beach in Los Angeles, where three times a week, DJs haul their gear out onto the sand and pass out headphones for self-identified dancers to move freely to music. Ecstatic dance is a form of dance in which the dancers, without the need to follow specific steps, abandon themselves to the rhythm and move freely as the music takes them. I found ecstatic dance early on in my creative journey, and it's become a staple of my own liberation practice. Every time I dance, it's a therapeutic moment between myself and the music. Creating space in your body through intentional movement has many benefits for your creativity, not to mention your general health and well-being.

Freewriting

Freewriting has been foundational for my own creative healing journey, as well as in my life as a professional artist. Everything written here in this book is a result of allowing my thoughts to flow from my brain to the page. I used to be so afraid when I sat down to write. I often experienced writer's block. I wouldn't know if I had anything to say, and all my Inner Overprotectors would burst in, reminding me that I had no idea what I was doing. It took a lot of commitment to create a freewriting practice. Eventually, the words started to flow.

I highly recommend "morning pages," which is a classic creativity practice shared by Julia Cameron in *The Artist's Way*. To complete your morning pages, simply sit down and write three pages of stream-of-consciousness thoughts every morning. And if you can't do it in the morning, then find some time later in the day to write three pages of whatever is flowing through your mind. These notes don't ever have to be looked at again, but they do help you tap into your ability to just flow with your thoughts and bring them out of your mind and onto the page.[2]

Be Time

Be time is the new me time. :) *Be time* is the space you carve out in which you are can flow with wherever your creativity wants you to go. This is your time to just be. You might think that in order to be a prolific artist, you need to take on a bunch of new projects and add a million more things to your to-do list. Actually, the opposite is true. The best thing you can do for your own creativity is to get very intentional about your be time. This isn't about productivity and more doing. It's about carving out that space in your calendar for you to be in flow. And in that time, if your creative impulse is to paint, draw, or write a new song, great! Or perhaps you'd like to practice yoga, gaze at yourself in the mirror, or fill a bath with flower petals and essential oils for a random midday soak. And, if all you want to do is lay around and dream on your couch, that's perfect too. Be time is unstructured space in your calendar for you to do whatever your heart desires.

If you are always focused on how much you produce, you're missing out on the huge gift that is cultivating your creativity and embodying your inner artist. The best part of being an artist is giving yourself lots of space to dream. I've seen it with my clients and with myself, over and over again—days and weeks of being too busy to find any time to access our creativity or be in flow. We long for pleasure and embodiment, but it's so easy to keep filling up that to-do list with more tasks, projects, and events so that we end up in a continuous cycle of burnout and recovery. If you find yourself in this place more than once, just know that you can always come back into realignment with your creative self.

It's very common for people to fill up every single space they have with obligations to other people, leaving nothing left for their own creativity. If you are always focusing on doing, without making space for you to be, you're going to end up feeling like a hamster on a hamster wheel. You won't feel fulfilled. And that longing to express your inner artist will constantly be pulling at you.

As humans, we have a need to just be with ourselves. We need to go deeper into our experience of life by making art about it. And the first step is being so present with our emotions and experiences that we are moved to create. You, my Radiant Wildheart, are so much more than just another cog in the machine of capitalism, meant to clock our hours, without any time to tune in to the deeper experience our inner artist wants us to have. So intentionally stop all the doing and striving, so that you can allow yourself to be moved.

Expansion Exercise

WILDHEARTIST DATE

A wildheartist date is a date with yourself and your inner artist. Remember, there is a romantic nature to courting your inner muses and seducing your inner artist so they want to show up in your life. This is a date that you go on by yourself. Pick a place that will inspire your creativity and allow yourself to flow once you are there. Here are some potential wildheartist dates:

- Museums
- Concert or a festival
- Yoga class
- Theater performance
- Bookstore
- Record shop
- Enjoying some unique architecture tours
- Art gallery
- Dance club
- Cooking class
- A hike to a scenic lookout point
- A forest hike
- A walk in a beautiful park with your journal or sketchbook
- Creative retreat

- Beach with your journal
- Stargazing
- Meditation center
- A café or garden where you can sketch your surroundings
- A walk around the city with your headphones and music
- A thrift shop
- Literally anything that sparks creativity within you

INNER OVERPROTECTOR

The Perfectionist

It's time to meet your inner Perfectionist. We all experience perfectionism in some way. This Inner Overprotector wants you to only share things that are fully completed to perfection. The Perfectionist is totally focused on the finished product and whether or not it will be deemed good enough. While you are creating, they consume your mind with thoughts and questions about how your creative expression will be received by your future imagined audience. In the mind of the Perfectionist, your future audience is full of harsh critics looking for any way to tear your work apart. Because of this, your Perfectionist doesn't have time to enjoy the process. They're too busy trying to protect you by fast-forwarding to the end result as quickly as possible. What might it mean if someone saw your work in progress and realized that it, and you, are not perfect?

If you allow yourself to be guided by the voice of your inner Perfectionist, it will take you out of the present moment and suck all the joy out of your creative practice. There are so many gifts to your creativity that you simply can't access when the Perfectionist is running the show, because the Perfectionist creates a very unpleasant experience out of your creativity. As a result, your creative practice becomes something you simply don't want to show up for.

At heart the Perfectionist wants you to be your best and holds you to an extremely high standard because this Inner Overprotector desperately wants to protect you from rejection or criticism.

You may be experiencing the Perfectionist if:

+ You've been feeling like you're "not ready" for a very long time.
+ You don't want to share your creative ideas or projects with others.
+ You want to skip over the process and just be at the end destination.
+ It takes you a long time to complete any project.
+ You don't give yourself the chance to try new things because you are afraid of not being good enough.

Tips for Dealing with the Perfectionist: Repeat this affirmation as often as you need to: *Everything is perfectly imperfect.* Remember that things that are perfect are boring, and it's actually the imperfections that make art interesting. Life is a little bit messy, and very few things are "perfect." Your art, too, can be both messy and beautiful at the same time. Notice areas in your life or your art where you feel you are "imperfect" and reframe negative feelings into feelings of gratitude. Gratitude is a very high vibration and will shift your energy immediately. Make a list

of all of the things you love about your art, and then take a moment to sit and breathe them in, actually receiving that gratitude into your body on a cellular level.

CREATIVE PRACTICE
5-Minute Art Assignments

Being consistent in your creative practice requires some devotion because, as we've uncovered, most of us are afraid to spend time with ourselves and our creativity. Once you understand why you are longing to embrace your creative practice, then you have to show up until it becomes second nature. Showing up is 75 percent of the battle. To help win that battle, try these short, quick, and easily accessible five-minute creative practices throughout the day.

As an art educator, I love creative assignments and prompts. I've given you some here to get yourself started, but you can earn bonus points by giving yourself spontaneous art assignments or even assigning some to your trusted allies who are also interested in growing their creativity. Make it a game and have fun with this process! Then notice as bigger and bigger creative breakthroughs start to come through.

Remember, these are just some options! You're invited to assign yourself your own five-minute creative practices that feel inspiring or aligned for you and your creative goals. Do these by yourself with no one around if that feels more comfortable. You can determine the pace at which you want to complete these assignments. Perhaps you want to start with just one per day. Or one every other day. If eventually you decide to do two or three in a day, I think you'll begin to feel very satisfied with your creative expansion. But the point of having these be short and sweet is to make your creativity ridiculously accessible, so it feels silly to not do it! The point is to break out of your routine and let yourself play so you can get all of that magical creative energy flowing again.

Dance

Put on one of your favorite songs and move your body intuitively. Close your eyes and follow what feels good and what kind of movements your body is asking for. Try to listen to your body. Jump around. Headbang. Shake it out and move any stagnant energy. And when you start to get too into your head, reconnect to your breath and touch your skin with your eyes closed. Find some time to yourself and put on headphones if you don't want people to hear your music. This is for you, not for anyone else. Let yourself flow with the music.

Writing

Write a love letter. Think of a person in your life that you absolutely adore. Someone who inspires you creatively and makes your heart sing. Light a candle and set up a sacred space for you to write them a love letter. This doesn't have to be a romantic letter, but simply putting words to your appreciation for this person and their essence in your life. You never have to give them this letter, but if it feels right or exciting, you can just to see what happens.

Music

Pick a song that you absolutely loved when you were younger. Pull up the lyrics and turn the volume up on your speaker. Have as much fun as you can singing the song and getting into character. Try adding to the experience by practicing replicating the dynamics of and the feeling behind the singer's voice. Explore your singing voice with no one watching and see if you can tap into the passion that the original artist meant to convey through this piece of music.

Expressive Arts

Create an image of your relationship to creativity in whatever medium or process speaks to you. It doesn't need to be pretty! Follow your intuition. Process over product. What's most important is the energy and feeling that you're putting into your creation. The end result does not matter, because your creativity is infinite. Don't judge your work as you create it. Be completely unattached to what it looks like and try to be spontaneous about your creative choices.

Archetype Spotlight

AMPLIFY YOUR CREATIVITY WITH MORE FLOW

 MYSTIC—Creative ideas float in the ethers, which means you're tapped into divine downloads that could become lots of different creative projects. Think of it like an endless stream of creativity that flows from your third eye to the stars. You can tap into this stream whenever you want to. These messages flow to you and are a gift bestowed from the Creative Spirit and your muses. It's up to you to choose which creative ideas you want to explore and place on your altar. Ask yourself, *What speaks to my heart the most strongly in this moment?* Trust and follow that.

VISIONARY—You tend to be a strong starter of projects but often don't see things through to completion. In the element of air, you desire to move very quickly. Because you see the bigger vision, you are prone to want to create it immediately. You might find yourself saying yes to all sorts of projects and then later feeling very overwhelmed and like an airy fairy. Remember that just because you see the vision doesn't mean that you need to get started on everything right now. Your vision might take one, two, or three years to execute and that's okay. What order of operations makes the most sense for you? Remember that you always need to give yourself the time and space to just *be* in addition to all of your amazing creative manifestations and *doing*. Every time you say yes to something, it takes up a little bit more of your bandwidth. So, make sure you are also saying a creative no to preserve your space and *be* time.

SACRED REBEL—With your fiery nature, you aren't afraid to be bold. But is there any part of you that is still shaming yourself for being too much? You are passionate, driven, and always thinking outside of the box. This means that a lot of the time, you're going to be pushing the edges of your and others' creativity. I want to encourage you to let yourself explore the things that might feel edgy for you or polarizing for others. No one needs to see this work but you. Give yourself permission to go there and explore your inner landscape with wild abandon. Why not? You only live once, right? The purpose of this is to stop shaming yourself for the ways you are different and embrace your wildness as a superpower. Sacred Rebel, you will never be too much. And when you take up all the space, you hold the torch for the rest of us to do the same.

 HEALER—Your creativity is what will ultimately heal you. When you create, you are creating for yourself and not for anyone else. Use your creative practices to tend to your inner child wounds. Let your creative practices soothe you. Whether you're journaling, posting on social media, or setting your intentions for a ceremony, choose to express yourself in ways that feel healing for you and your inner child. This is the gift that your cooling watery nature brings to you through your creativity. And beloved, if it heals you, it will profoundly help others too. Transmute everything that you are feeling and make art about it. Alchemize it on the proverbial canvas. Never shame yourself for your depth and sensitivity because these are absolutely your greatest assets that make you such a dynamic and profound artist. You are the Healer, and you speak to our hearts in a way that no one else can.

GUARDIAN—Make no mistake about it, you are highly creative and a brilliant artist. The only problem is that you hold yourself to such a high standard that it seems like it takes forever for you to finally share your creativity, and be seen in it. You're our Guardian, and to do so, you are naturally so grounded and logical that sometimes you're not as willing to put yourself out on a limb and take risks of being seen, especially if you don't feel like what you're sharing is perfect or "done." Let's be honest: you struggle with perfectionism and as soon as you acknowledge that, you'll be able to take the steps to break through it so you can spark your creative revolution. When you share your creations and are witnessed in them, you'll start to embody yourself as an artist even more. Let your hair down and allow yourself to be perfectly imperfect. Let us see you in your process. Get a little messy and share your work long before it's complete. Remember, the point of your creativity is to get liberated, *not* to have a beautifully finished product.

CHAPTER EIGHT

Pleasure

Let Your Deepest Desires Lead the Way

The sun is just peaking over the mountains as I roll over in my bed to snooze my alarm. I might sleep in for another five minutes, or maybe I'll indulge in another hour of dreamy rest. It's anyone's guess. I'm cozy, warm, and naked as I notice the light pouring through my windows. A symphony of birds are chirping as I appreciate the way the wind moves all the trees that surround my home. They're casting shadows on the wall that dance with my breath and I revel in the beauty of another moment to feel alive and grateful for all of the beauty that I've manifested in my life.

At first, I wasn't sure if I was worthy of this dreamy, fairy cathedral. It's nestled on a hilltop in the Santa Monica Mountains, and I had never rented a place so beautiful or expansive. Prior to this, I was squeezing my life into a 500-square-foot studio. But once the pandemic hit, I knew I needed space to hold all my dreams, and for right now, this is the per-fect location—tucked into a canyon, eight minutes from the beach. You'd never know that all of Los Angeles is right outside my doorstep because it feels so idyllic. I've been glad I said yes to this space, even when I didn't know if I could afford it. My thinking was, if it made me feel more abun-dant, then yes, it was completely worth it. And that's proven to be true.

I touch my skin and admire the sensory experience of the deep-red silk sheets I invested in. Worth every penny. Even if there's no one in the bed but me. After luxuriating in my bed for as long as I please, I decide that today is a day in which I will be devoted to my practices. Yesterday I might have fallen off the wagon, but today I'm ready to indulge in giving myself all of the time and space that I need to welcome pleasure into every cell of my being before starting my workday.

I am here to play

Not every day is like this, but I try to find at least a couple of days a week where I can spend plenty of time doing whatever my heart desires. I listen for what my body and soul want and give myself the world and anything that I want.

Today, I want to wake up without an alarm clock, and I take my sweet time getting out of bed. I want to intentionally make a yummy breakfast and dance around my kitchen to songs that turn me all the way on, dropping low into my hips to give myself a much-needed stretch and opening. I slither and slide around my home, following wherever my intuition takes me. I've got nowhere to be but here because I've set my life up so that I can have many mornings like this—with ample space to go slow and listen to my wants and needs in the moment. I've set up my schedule and my business, so I don't have any appointments till 11 A.M. at the earliest, but usually it's much later than that. Because doing whatever I want in the morning makes me feel alive. And I can easily fill up four hours in the morning with a juicy series of morning practices that nourish and ground me, so I can serve at my highest level and feel inspired in every cell of my body. And that trickles out into my Creative Mission.

I immediately make my way onto the floor. My yoga mat is already set up, and I crawl over to it because I'm committed to getting in my stretches that keep me feeling expansive in my body. I play music with a deep bass line. One that makes me want to gyrate my hips and stretch all the way out. Most days, I hardly feel like myself without taking some time to intentionally move my body. To purposefully connect to my breath, and remember that I incarnated at this time on planet Earth for a reason. And the more freedom I feel in my vessel, the more space I have to hold all of my creative genius. I do a yoga routine that is entirely intuitively guided, listening to my body as she speaks to me and tells me what she wants.

I trust myself to lead my pleasure practice in exactly the perfect way. It doesn't take long for my yoga session, maybe 20 minutes or so. I've been practicing since I was a teenager, with several teacher trainings under my belt, so I let my body be my guide, trusting that she knows what to do. I enjoy a juicy Savasana so I can reap all the benefits of my practice before I pull up a meditation app on my phone. Meditation is something that I sometimes resist, so I let it be extra easy and accessible. I choose a five-minute guided session that includes poetry by Rumi, my favorite poet. I play it on my loudspeaker with no worries about who will hear me. They'll enjoy the poetry too, I'm sure. The frequency I'm cultivating is good for the planet. I revel in Rumi's words as it inspires messages of eternal love into my heart. I'm reminded of what's true, embracing my soul's belonging in this divine mystery. I don't always get the chance to meditate, but today, I send myself waves of celebration because I gave that to myself.

From there, I reach for my journal. I have so many of them strewn throughout my house. They all serve different purposes, but I find that handwriting is the best way for me to access my Intuitive Higher Self and clear out the gunk. I jot down a few notes of what I'm grateful for today and then begin furiously writing. It's all a stream of consciousness, and sometimes it's just straight-up scribbles. I practice letting my thoughts flow into my morning pages. I know that no matter what I write, it's healing me on some level. So I let it all out. No matter how messy or illegible. I just keep going until I've hit three pages or 10 minutes, whichever comes first.

I let my thoughts flow onto the page without thinking or judging my writing. Here, in my journal, I spend time with myself. These are notes that no one will read. It's full of my fears, my dreams, and any random thoughts that want to be expressed. I'm noticing what's there without judgment and giving myself space to express what I'm feeling.

When I was younger, my parents and sibling used to search my room to try and read my journal, and my deepest thoughts would be exposed. I would hide my notebook between the mattress where no one could find it. But I don't have to do that anymore. I don't have to hide. I explore whatever is on my mind and let myself go there. No editing. It's illuminating because I get to see exactly what is taking up precious real estate in my subconscious. Usually, what pours out is unexpected. But that's perfect. Because I'm always leaning in with curiosity about what will show up on today's pages.

It's time to nourish myself. Most mornings, I start my day with a simple and healthy smoothie. It's classic and easy to make, full of fruits and superfoods, and I always make sure to add a little extra sea moss that I process myself. As I pour it into the blender, reveling in its smooth and luxurious texture, I appreciate myself for taking the time to prepare something that my body loves. I honor myself for tending to my body, which holds all of the magic and wisdom that allows me to make an impact in the world. I'm grateful for me. Once my smoothie is made, it's time to party.

I bump some music as loud as I can on my speaker and dance all over the open floor plan of my house. The music I play has lots of bass and tribal beats that command me to move as intentionally as I can. I'm shaking my hips and dropping them down low, stretching and releasing any stagnant energy I might be storing. I let myself be wild, twerking my hips to find that much more freedom in my root chakra. I learned so much in all the erotic dance classes that I took about how to release shame somatically. I move like a snake, taking extra effort to go as slow as possible, connecting with my deepest breaths, and touching my skin sensually. I let out an audible exhale that helps me feel present and connected to my wild primal self. I let out a roar filled with all of the stagnant energy that I've been holding on to. I shake my entire body, letting everyone's expectations and energy fall all the way off me. And once I feel clear, I'm ready to get to work.

It's 11:11 A.M. when my calendar app dings with a notification that it's time for my daily sacred music ritual. I popped it into my calendar because it's something I usually put off. My current intention as an artist is to expand myself as a musician and DJ, to express myself creatively through sound and performance. So, I decided that for five days a week, I will show up to my music practice as a sacred ritual no matter what. I put it in my calendar because I've found that what's in my calendar always seems to get done. When this alarm rings, I make sure to turn my phone on Do Not Disturb and put it away where it can't distract me. The last thing I need is Instagram notifications buzzing and the temptation of endless content to keep me from showing up to what's most important to me right now.

I'm learning a new DJ software, and today my goal is to dig around for music and add to my digital collection. I know that eventually this will turn into my first DJ mix, but I've made it a point to not focus on that. While it's easy to always be thinking about the end result or output, in my sacred music ritual, I want to focus on having fun only. When I focus on the end result, it tends to suck all the magic right out of my creative practice. It puts me back in that mindset of caring about what everyone else is going to think. It feels contrived. But when I let myself be present to how much fun I'm having, letting the music move me and dancing to the vibes that I'm curating for myself, it's an unbeatably lovely way to start my workday.

After my music ritual, I have 30 minutes of unscheduled time where I can do anything I please. This is on the calendar because I know myself. I am someone who loves breaks. Nothing makes me feel more abundant than having lots of space to be free. I make it a point to incorporate lots of breaks between all my meetings so that I never feel rushed or over-whelmed by back-to-back Zoom meetings. I love having time to myself. Today I decide to FaceTime my current bae and flirt it up for a moment before they head to work. It feels so luxurious to spend this time connecting with those juicy, flirty feelings in the middle of the day. Yum!

Finally, it's time for my first meeting. It's a Tuesday, and I am scheduled for some coaching calls with clients. I absolutely adore these calls, and they hardly feel like work at all. Today's meeting is with a client named Lua. When she first met me, she didn't have a business at all and was doing under-the-table work that didn't make her feel fully empowered. But when Lua saw what I was doing, she wanted that level of freedom for herself too. So she hired me to teach her how to grow a creative business that sets her free. Now she works for herself on her own schedule and has grown a magical platform teaching spirituality and plant medicines to magical beings that see and appreciate her.

Lua is sustaining herself fully through her soul's work. She's learning the energetics of how to hold boundaries with her clients and enroll people into programs she's created entirely out of her creativity. She is so grateful for my presence in her life, because she never knew this was possible for her. This call was as nourishing for Lua as it was for me. I took it while lounging on a fuzzy white rug in my living room, stretching in between giving her advice on her business and reflecting back to her what she sounds most excited about. I'm pinching myself that I get paid to do this work. For so many years, I would have done this for free.

The rest of my day is full of more powerful meetings with beautiful people who are doing deep healing work on themselves as they create world-changing businesses. As I show up to each meeting, I am relaxed, confident, and excited to reflect back to my students their strengths and power. I don't feel like I need to show up any way other than how I am. I'm fully in my pleasure and liberated in my life. I live on purpose, and that's why these people have chosen me as their mentor.

Finally, it's time to lead my group-coaching call for the Muse Business Academy, my business mentorship program. On the call, I hear life-changing breakthroughs from student after student. One just signed their first client, another just led their first online event, and another is planning their first retreat. There's so much excitement that we end the call with celebrations, wins, and brags. Everyone has such amazing things to celebrate. Afterward, my inbox overflows with messages of gratitude from students. On some level, I can't believe that this is my job. But I put so much intentionality and creative manifestation powers into creating this life and making this my reality.

When I was in high school, I was the girl who barely graduated. I got D's and F's on my report card and regularly intercepted the daily mail to prevent my parents from finding my detention slips and progress reports. Most adults in my life assumed that I wasn't going anywhere. But when I got to college, I was encouraged to choose my own course of study. So I picked classes that sounded interesting with topics that I had always wanted to learn about. I studied visual art, art history, psychology, and sociology. I wrote papers on topics that truly inspired me and that I wanted to learn more about.

Once I started to lead with pleasure, I found out that I'm actually not a terrible student or a failure. In fact, I love to learn. And, perhaps even more surprising, I love to teach. I was a freshman in college when I suddenly became a straight A student for the first time. I started a radio show and led campus clubs. I published the school newspaper, which I helped turn into a handmade zine filled with art and poetry.

Pleasure connects me to what's possible. Pleasure keeps me attuned to my body and wanting to show up for more. Pleasure creates a force field around me that nourishes my life with lots of juice. It gives me more capacity. And the more I prioritize my pleasure, the more magic I create in the world.

Like so many people, I struggled to prioritize my pleasure because I thought it made me selfish or ungrateful. But now I know that pleasure is revolutionary. So many of our ancestors sacrificed their desires in the name of tradition. For me to go out there as a queer first-generation Muslim-American woman of color and declare that I wanted to dance, sing, and grow a creative revolutionary business where I prioritized my pleasure was nerve-wracking. But since then, I've learned how life-changing it is to embrace my desires. The people who came before me sacrificed so that today, I could be a divine embodiment of radical self-expression. And I am already seeing how the younger generations that come after me are living with so much less shame and so much more freedom.

Bit by bit, as I chip away layers of shame and trauma, I find more space to hold these juicy, pleasurable feelings. And every time I do, I remember that my liberation is medicine for the planet. So I use pleasure as my north star. Because by living my own personal revolution, I am doing my part to create the world that I've always wanted to see. One where we can live free to be ourselves. I pray to my muses to let my renaissance be a wild party filled with joy and laughter. Let it be sexy. Let it be intentional. Let it be filled with music and art. As I dream it into being, I create a life that's aligned to my truth—the environment that I always needed. And if it heals me, I know it will help others too.

Teaching

YOUR PLEASURE EXISTS IN MULTITUDES

Pleasure is anything that makes you feel good. When many people think of the word *pleasure*, they immediately veer toward sexuality. Of course, sexuality is a delicious aspect of pleasure, but it's far from the whole picture. Pleasure encompasses sexuality and also goes so far beyond that. If you limit your experience of pleasure to just sex, then you're missing out on the infinite ways that pleasure can enhance every other area of your life too.

Your senses are what open the doorway to experiencing more pleasure in your life. When you stop, tune in, and live from all your senses, you open up to the full extent of the pleasure that's available to you in every moment. Have you embraced your sensual side? In order to do so, you have to slow all the way down to appreciate the moments that we often take for granted. Feeling the fabric of your clothes touching your skin, moving your body to music, and eating yummy foods can all help you access your pleasurable and sensual energy. Tuning in to your pleasure will bring you feelings of joy, bliss, and ecstasy. And who doesn't want more of that? When you're in these very high vibrational states, you greatly enhance your ability to express yourself fully in the world. Pleasure is often the missing piece.

Pleasure expands your ability to receive. Receiving is a practice. The more you open yourself to receiving the yumminess that life has to offer, the more you will be able to experience bliss and fulfillment right now. Whether you're talking about love, sex, money, or joy, tapping into your pleasure energy will help you magnetize more abundance into your life because it increases your capacity. If ever any of my clients are feeling overwhelmed, my question is always, "How can you bring more pleasure into your day?" This always helps their mental wellness and ability to manage whatever they've got going on.

When you're not actively in a pleasure practice and used to receiving, chances are that you're going to unconsciously block or self-sabotage the blessings and opportunities that the universe wants to send your way. This might look like deflecting compliments when people tell you how magical you are. Or perhaps you are afraid to forge new relationships with people who express interest in you. Or maybe you just can't let positive feedback from others sink in and resonate. Or you might just feel so overwhelmed that you don't notice all of the positive changes that you're making. The more you spend time intentionally cultivating your pleasure practice, the more you'll be able to welcome and receive everything that you're calling in. In your quest to be fully expressed and create a life that turns you on, pleasure will be your guiding light.

Pleasure is medicine. If you want to bring forth your Creative Mission, it's absolutely essential for you to get connected with your pleasure. Your relationship with your pleasure is holy and deeply spiritual because it allows you to be more tuned in to the subtle energies that are moving you and connecting you to the feeling of being truly alive. Being connected with your pleasure will heal the parts of yourself that feel shame.

Your desires are sacred. There is nothing wrong with claiming them boldly and allowing them to come to you. There is nothing wrong with expressing your feelings. Acknowledging your truth is sacred, and something that so many of our ancestors were not able to do. In a world that tells you who you should be, your pleasure will show you who you truly are. It isn't something that you let yourself indulge in every once in a while, but an everyday and every moment practice that will liberate your creative spirit. Your pleasure will activate your imagination and allow you to become a fully expressed divine being who can easily spark a revolution.

THE WITCH WOUND

For centuries, women who were intimately connected to their sovereign nature and their ability to experience pleasure were seen as witches. In fact, as an art history major, I learned that the earliest depictions of witches were nude women who were dancing together without a man present. What was so threatening about these women that they were later labeled as witches?

What was it about these women's sensual sovereignty, pleasure, and magic that was seen as such a threat? Well, the status quo was that a woman would marry a man, the husband would buy or inherit land, and the couple would tend to it. If these women were able to exist in their pleasure without a man present, it could topple all of society as we knew it! #Patriarchymuch? Later women who were connected with their intuition and psychic gifts were labeled as witches and barbarically burned at the stake in front of a crowd of people. This sent the message that if you chose your individuality and to pursue your unique gifts, you were putting yourself at grave risk. In fact, most women who were labeled "different" in any way at all were persecuted for it.

Today we are all still carrying this wound. It shows up in our society when pleasure-centered beings, mostly femmes, are slut shamed or victim blamed. It shows up when we are afraid to be seen in our sensual power. It shows up when we feel like we need to sacrifice essential parts of ourselves in order to be accepted in the world.

The oppressive nature of shame has been a tool of the patriarchy since the beginning of Western civilization. So if you're feeling like it's difficult to open up and receive pleasure, know that you're not alone. If you're feeling afraid of what might happen if you claim your desires and lead with your sensuality, and you're not even sure where that fear comes from, remember that what you're experiencing is not just your own. We have all inherited this witch wound, and it's been passed down to us for generations.

Much of what you are feeling is the burden of being the ancestral Healer in your lineage. You're carrying the pain of those who came before you as you take these steps to finally heal it so that it doesn't continue after you. Progressively releasing all of that fear and shame will help heal the collective wound we all experienced, so future generations can live with so much more freedom to express. Your pleasure is a revolution, and Wildhearts across the world are here to witness and celebrate you in it in every way.

MASTER THE ART OF HAVING FUN

It's time to feel amazing and fabulous, so you can truly give from a wildly overflowing cup. When you do, you can luxuriate and rest easy in the knowledge that liberating your pleasure is a service to the planet and essential for you to live from your Creative Mission.

So many of us treat our creative practices like another job. We are taught that the only valuable way to spend our time is by being productive. In the United States, work and productivity are the top priorities. I have definitely been guilty of this. I was always focused on the end game. What would be the result? A finished painting to show? An album? A book? A new program that I could launch? A certain amount of money or recognition? I wanted something I could share with the world to say, "I am here. See me."

But when you focus on the finished product, your mind immediately starts fixating on what others will think of what you are creating. If you approach your creativity the way you do other work, you'll easily fall into the traps of your Inner Overprotectors. If you believe that others will judge you or won't approve, you'll end up judging yourself for following your bliss and doing what feels right for you. And then the cycle just continues to repeat itself and creates a self-fulfilling prophecy where you long to be doing what truly calls to you, but you still aren't.

The key is to focus instead on having fun. Sounds simple enough, but actually setting your intention to have as much fun as possible while you create is wildly profound. When you aren't having fun in your process, you might find that you battle your own resistance every step of the way. You'll complain more and emphasize the things that aren't working or don't make you feel good. You might find that your mind is elsewhere and you're not as present. You may notice yourself saying that you're bored.

In contrast, when you set your intention on having more fun in your creative practice, you can be fully present in the process of expressing yourself. You'll be filled with a greater sense of imagination. New ideas will flow from you that otherwise wouldn't be there. You'll be more enthusiastic, which will be infectious for the people you're working with. Being excited by what you're doing will give you the drive to show up fully for it. Laughter, pleasure, and bliss are at the top of the list for what keeps us mentally resilient and able to show up for the hard work of getting liberated and embodying our Radiant Wildheart energy. And it doesn't hurt that it's absolutely magnetic, and we will all want to be in your energetic field when you are emitting those pleasure-filled fun vibes. If you want to spark a movement, make sure that we get to see you absolutely loving what you do. Then we will want to join you.

Centering fun is a constant practice, one that you may need to remind yourself of often. Your creativity can be the most liberating and fun thing in the world, so give yourself permission to enjoy it. When you find yourself getting into your head, recenter your intentions to being present. Notice what feels delicious and do more of that. Tune out distractions and be present with yourself as you have a blast in whatever you are doing. The more fun you have, the more you will be able to create something amazing. And when you love it, a natural result is that others will too.

CREATIVE PRACTICE

Deep Desires

So often, when I ask my students what it is they want for themselves, they look puzzled. You'd be amazed at how many people are walking this planet without ever having stopped to inquire this. Wildheart, what do you desire? Do you even know? Could you put words to it? Don't worry if you don't have the words yet because you are not alone. Most Wildhearts that I talk to need some coaching to really name and claim their desires and advocate for what they want and need in this lifetime. And for those who have and know the answer, often they're just barely scratching the surface out of fear of wanting too much or taking up too much space with their desires. But that doesn't mean that those desires aren't there. Claiming your desires is a practice, and an important one.

Your desires are electric. You might be hearing a call where there's something on your mind that you can't stop thinking about. You probably feel an unexplainable longing. You might find yourself fantasizing and daydreaming about something. Maybe you've even got some shame around it, like *Who am I to want something this radical or amazing?* Your desires could be in any area of your life. Perhaps it's a certain type of relationship, a home, a feeling, or an accomplishment. There is absolutely no limit to your desires and no reason to hold them back. I invite you to explore them and let yourself dream into what would feel the most revolutionary. Give yourself permission to go there, as if nothing were off-limits. Don't worry about what's taboo or what other people might think. Just be curious and see where your desires take you.

Oftentimes, we shame ourselves for our desires. You might tell yourself that you can't have the things that you want. You might project judgment onto yourself based on what you think others will say about your desires. But I think all feelings and desires are beautiful. They are human. And there is never anything to be ashamed of for how you feel. Shame comes from a place of lack. If you have been telling yourself that you can't have what you want, you are trapped in a lie that is not serving your empowerment or most authentic expression. Who cares what anyone else thinks about your desires? And even if you don't have what you want now, by acknowledging what they are, you can begin to create a life that is more honest and aligned to what your spirit is calling in. When you let yourself explore your deepest desires without shame so you can understand *why* you are longing for those things, you can begin to orient yourself like a compass to point exactly toward what you want and take inspired action in that direction as often as you can.

In the following exercise, you are going to shamelessly declare your desires to yourself and to the universe. Then you're going to set time aside to intentionally connect with your longing, to feel it in your body and in your senses without guilt or shame. Once you've accessed these feelings, you're going to find out how your desires connect to your Creative Mission so that you never doubt or hide from what you want again. When you know how your deepest desires play into the bigger picture of what you are creating with your life, you will be less likely to compromise on them.

1. Write out a list of five of your deepest desires.

2. Say more: Go through each of your deep desires and write out a paragraph about why you are longing for each of these things.

3. Meditate on each of these desires. Feel the longing in your body. Where do you feel this desire? Taste, touch, hear, see, and feel it. Breathe into it, move with it, connect to it.

4. If this feels good and luscious for you, write five more desires, and repeat steps 2 and 3.

5. Consider your past and the challenges that you've moved through in your Divine Purpose Path. Explore how these desires relate to your personal healing and liberation journey. If we teach what we most need to learn, try to journal about how being honest about your desires and owning these parts of yourself proudly relate to your Creative Mission in the world as you know it. Do you want to help other people access those feelings too? Why or why not?

INNER OVERPROTECTOR

The Martyr

Meet the Martyr. The Martyr is your Inner Overprotector that tells you in order to be a good person, you have to sacrifice your needs. The voice of the Martyr can be quite melodramatic. It tells you that you need to run yourself to the ground to accomplish your goals or be a true activist in the world. I have worked with many activists, community organizers, and people in the nonprofit sector. Often the sentiment among them is that one needs to work themselves around the clock in order to make an impact. This means that self-care is often at the bottom of the priority list because there's much more "important" work that needs to be done.

When you're ruled by the Martyr, you feel burned out and depleted. Usually, this exhaustion is coupled with negative thoughts and low self-worth. Many people learn the Martyr because we are told that our productivity is what makes us valuable or because we've been taught that we need to put others' needs before our own. The Martyr links your worth with your accomplishments, including how much you do and sacrifice for others. It tells you that to put your needs first is selfish or morally questionable. But I believe that if everyone made sure their own needs were met first, then we would have much healthier and happier relationships with one another.

You might be experiencing the Martyr if:

- ✦ You feel like your deep desires aren't worthy of your time.
- ✦ You think you need to sacrifice in order to be a good person.
- ✦ You put everyone else's needs before your own.
- ✦ You only feel like your work is valuable if it's correlated with your making money.
- ✦ You don't have time to pursue your passions.
- ✦ You're feeling depleted and burned out.

Expansion Exercise

PLEASURE ACTIVATION PRACTICE

You don't have to wait any longer to allow yourself to feel the sensual and pleasurable energy that will enhance every area of your life. It doesn't matter what gender you are or how you identify, slowing down to deepen your sensory experience will allow you to find more presence and safety in your body. You can expand your pleasure field right now by accessing one of the following pleasure-activation practices. If having a pleasure-centered attitude doesn't come naturally to you, that's okay! This expansion exercise is here to make pleasure more and more accessible to you by taking small steps toward increasing your capacity to feel and hold it.

No matter how busy you might be, your pleasure-activation practice is always here to weave in bits of pleasure throughout your day to help you incrementally increase your ability to hold more goodness and magic that you will radiate out through your Creative Mission. These expansion exercises are meant to help make those yummy feelings more readily available to you at any moment of the day. If you are just starting out with opening up to your radiant pleasure energy, only do this activation practice once per day. As you get more comfortable, try having two pleasure activations per day. Once that feels easy and comfortable, increase it to three times a day. Keep going until your entire day feels like a fabulous festival of healing energy and lovely vibes.

The beauty of these pleasure activations is that you can do them anywhere and they only take five minutes. You can do them while you are stuck in traffic, getting ready for bed, or during a lull in your workday. As you keep incrementally increasing your pleasure energy, you'll also increase your ability to hold and receive pleasure. This will help you amplify your abundance and magnetize way more magic into your life.

Pleasure Activation: Set a timer for at least five minutes and do something completely devoted to pleasure during that time. This can look absolutely any way that you want. Five minutes is a great starting point, and something that you can do even if you work outside of the home. My pleasure practice can sometimes take hours, but it started with me taking five minutes here and there. The beauty of the five-minute container is that it feels so accessible. You can do anything for five minutes, right? And once you get started, if you feel inclined to add another five minutes, then follow your bliss and go for it!

The following is a list of some pleasure-activation practices that you can do. This is by no means a comprehensive list. Feel free to try any of them, but remember that the whole point is to make sure that your pleasure practice feels good for you. If any of these activities don't bring you joyous, sensuous feelings, perhaps it's not right for you now. And that's totally okay! The last thing I want is for this practice to turn into work or another task on your endless to-do list. The most important thing is that you tap into your pleasure intentionally and more often so that you can see how it revolutionizes your life and creativity.

Five-Minute Pleasure Practice Ideas

+ Eat something decadent.

+ Self-administer a massage and touch your skin.

+ Take your time putting body oil on while listening to positive affirmation music, such as Beautiful Chorus, Toni Jones, or Londrelle.

+ Sing a song that you used to love when you were a preteen or teenager.

+ Buy yourself flowers.

+ Have a sensual moment with yourself and any one of your senses.

+ Tidy your physical space with intention.

+ Journal or have your morning practice, and start your day with an intentional moment by yourself.

+ Anoint yourself with herbal sprays or essential oils.

+ Dance like no one's watching.

+ Trace a rose or flower over your skin.

+ Wear clothes that feel sensual to you.

+ Practice breathwork.

+ Get cozy and meditate.

+ Pull an oracle card.

+ Color a page in a coloring book.

+ Go outside and get some sunshine.

And if you have more than five minutes, here are a few more pleasure practices that are well worth the time to revel in your sensual nature!

+ Read a novel just for fun.

+ Have a luxurious bath-time ritual.

+ Grocery shop, letting pleasure lead the way for your purchases.

+ Go for a walk through your neighborhood.

+ Take an erotic dance class.

+ Take yourself on a date! Go to a fancy restaurant, the movies, or a museum.

+ Treat yourself to something you've been wanting.

+ Spend some time in nature.

+ Sleep in later than you normally would.

Archetype Spotlight

REMEMBER PLEASURE IN EVERY MOMENT

 MYSTIC—Ether tends to bring out your serious side. But there's something so divine about your ability to play and express yourself like the wild fairy that you are. By connecting to your pleasure, you can remember how to have fun and play more, which will unlock all sorts of silly sides to your self-expression. Mystical one, let yourself laugh, giggle, and lighten up! Try on some costumes and see what kind of alter egos you might be able to access. Why not? Life is short!

 VISIONARY—Your thoughts move as quickly as the air, and as such, you have so many wonderful ideas you wish to pursue. But you should only go after the ones that sound like fun to you! If it isn't fun, then what's the point? You're going to show up with so much more dynamism if you're doing something that absolutely turns you on. So let yourself be drawn to the things you find beautiful. If you're wondering which option to go with, follow the one that sounds the most simple, easy, and fun.

 SACRED REBEL—You are someone who pursues your pleasure naturally and often, and that's a powerful thing. Like the fire, it's your passion that fans your flames, and it's absolutely magnetic . . . and frankly, very sexy too! However, remember that you need to be mindful of others around you as you pursue your own pleasure. How can you lift others up with you on your fiery pursuit of your passions without burning bridges? How can you let us into your passion so we can join you on your Creative Mission? Let us feel you and all of your heat, because it sparks something inside of us too.

HEALER—Like the drops of water running down your skin, you are just oozing sensuality. If you practice, you'll find that you are naturally comfortable in states of flow, pleasure, and play. The more you let yourself be in your flow state, the more your creativity will begin to overflow all over your life. Make sure that you do your pleasure practices so that you can get out of your mind and into your body's wisdom. And share this passion and yummy energy with the people in your life, because your energy is surely going to be medicine for them too. You're a catalyst that will inspire others to be more pleasure centered and in flow too.

 GUARDIAN—You have a natural tendency toward the sensual. Embrace it. How can you create a more earthly sensory experience in your day-to-day life? Think of the fabrics you wear, the foods you eat, and the activities you participate in. Let yourself luxuriate in it. Get as comfy and cozy as you can. Indulge. The more that your day reflects your sensual nature, the more pleasure and receptivity you'll be able to tap into.

CHAPTER NINE

Healing

Become Your Own Healer
and Pave the Way for Others

My favorite space used to be my seventh grade visual-arts classroom. The room was airy, with high ceilings and lots of light coming in through big windows. I remember learning how to use acrylic paints in that classroom, the medium that now, for me, feels like home. But as a sense of home often does, painting brings up complicated emotions for me. To this day, when I stare at a blank canvas, I am confronted with all my deepest fears and insecurities. And at the same time, I'm totally turned on.

A blank canvas represents the infinite possibility of what could happen next. But when I was younger, like in my seventh-grade classroom, all I felt was the fear. I remember trying to get my teacher to paint my painting for me. The stakes just felt so high. One wrong move, I thought, and this painting might as well go into the trash. All I wanted was to create something that I felt was beautiful. Something that inspired me like all of the other art that moved me from some place inside. Something I could hang on my wall, or better yet, that maybe my parents would be proud enough to hang on their wall. I was terrified to mess it up and fairly certain that I didn't have the technical skills for the job.

So being ever resourceful and committed to seeing my vision through in one way or another, I employed a strategy that I then employed often.

Find someone else, a better artist, a more creative thinker, someone with more talent to execute it for me. Do you ever do this? Seek the answers from outside of yourself? Ask everyone around you what they would do, how they would respond, or what they think of a given creative challenge.

I remember emphatically raising my hand to grab the attention of Ms. Cris, my middle school art teacher. She was my icon, and I wanted to be just like her when I grew up—effortlessly cool and stylish, and she actually treated us like adults. Her class was easily the most fun, and we had full permission to roam about the room and do what we needed while she blasted music. Her arts classroom was a vibe. I called her to my desk that day with a secret agenda. I wanted her to paint the most important part of my painting for me because she would do it better. And I wanted my art to be *good* (I now loathe using this word when describing art). I positioned my easel and paintbrush just so, so that she could easily grab it and make the marks for me. She took my cue, and I exhaled a sigh of relief. My painting might be salvageable after all.

Fifteen years later, I'm reminded of those exact same feelings while teaching my own visual arts class in South Central Los Angeles. I had finally landed a job as an elementary school art teacher, and I was teaching a visual arts lesson of my own.

In the moment I recognize that on some level I—and probably my inner child—am nervous. There's a fear in the back of my mind that I'm not a good enough artist to lead this lesson or anyone in finding their creativity. My Inner Overprotectors are going off, telling me that perhaps this will finally be the place where I will be found out. As a fraud. A poser. A wannabe artist. But my students are simply excited to have a creative experience with me. They look up to me the same way that I looked up to Ms. Cris. They're endlessly interested in me and every mark that I make. They're in awe, wondering how I got so confident and are mesmerized by my ability to draw. Although I still feel like an inadequate draftsperson, they don't seem to notice or care. They love my classroom, and it's obvious that it's their favorite place to be.

Samari is an adorable six-year-old with big brown eyes and shaggy hair. Like me at his age, he has a history of behavioral issues that has most of his teachers treating him like he's a problem student. In most of his classes, he gets in trouble a lot for talking out of turn or not listening enough. But not here.

I see him as a different type of thinker, a creative who needs to have his gifts and strengths nurtured. He raises his hand to call me over to his desk where his half-finished work of art sits. He doesn't realize that I am picking up his internal dialogue just by reading his body language. His paper and oil pastel are already tilted toward me as he asks for help. It would probably be faster and easier for me to just paint it for him, since several other students also need my attention. But I can tell that something deeper is going on here. Although he puts on a tough exterior, Samari's creativity is just as fragile and precious as anyone else's.

I know these feelings all too well, and now I recognize how beautifully human they are. After years of studying the creative process, I know there's the potential for real healing here. He doesn't need me to draw the line, because what good would that do? If I draw it for him, it will only put a temporary bandage over his sacred creative wound. This wound, if not fully healed, could potentially haunt him into his adulthood like it does for so many of the Wildhearts that I meet! Not on my watch.

What would really help him grow as an artist is to hold a supportive and lighthearted space for him to muster his bravery and try it on his own. To create something that's uniquely his, an imprint that no one else could make. That's what will make his artwork beautiful and so much more interesting than if I did it for him.

On a separate piece of paper, I show him what I would do and explain how he can do it himself. How simple and fun it could be. I encourage him, staying by his side as he picks up his brush and remaining reassuring that he's definitely got this. Samari goes for it, drawing big eyes on his owl painting. He adds some flair and personality by adding long exaggerated lashes. The eyes of his owl stare back at his own, and we all smile with excitement. What he's created is special and filled with his energy. I'm proud of him, but more importantly, he's proud of himself and what he's created. And at the end of the day, as his art teacher, that's all that matters.

The lessons that I learned as an art teacher are still the foundation of what I do today. I had the privilege of witnessing the creative process in children and adults from every walk of life. And no matter what age you are, the process of unleashing your inner artist is the same. I saw over and over again the moment that children go from being wild and free to becoming more self-conscious and critical of themselves. I witnessed how often those creative blocks remain there until they are intentionally broken through. Until someone chooses to heal their sacred creative wound and push past the voices of those Inner Overprotectors.

We aren't born with the fear of making mistakes. We develop that fear somewhere along the way. As my students got older, for example, they became more resistant to painting outside of the lines and expressing themselves with wild abandon. They became more aware of the perceived judgments and comparison to their peers. They were more concerned with how their work of art looked rather than what they felt like while they were creating it. And they became less willing to be seen in their imperfections. Our self-expression is so precious and meaningful, and to share our authentic selves and not have it be received well is a huge risk that so many of us are unwilling to take.

I'd seen it in my classroom, and I experienced it myself since I was their age. And no matter how much I heal my sacred creative wound, every new aspect of my liberation comes with its own layers of resistance to break through. For example, when I first told my coming-out story online, it was a whole new level of vulnerability for me. I had never shared those parts of my story and how it all made me feel with so much candidness, let alone for the whole world to see. I was constantly afraid of my family of origin, seeing it and judging me all over again. It sent my inner child into a panic. I had gotten used to hiding in anonymity where certain people couldn't find me.

But once I got more visible, I knew that I had no choice but to fully come out in every sense of the word. My Creative Mission demanded it from me. And even though it was hard, my liberation was on the other side. And that, for me, is priceless and my priority in this lifetime.

When I first started writing this book, my writing mentor SARK told me that her hope was that I cry all over these pages. She told me that my book was writing me, but at the time, I didn't understand what she meant. This work of art that you are holding in your hands has taken me over four years of struggle, procrastination, and wanting to throw it all away and never look at it again. It has taken me this long to be able to write honestly—to tell my story and to know in my bones that it matters because I have something irreplaceable to contribute to the world.

At first, I couldn't write anything. The blank page would make me feel stuck. I would blank out at the computer, feeling miserable for hours. I would show up to my mentorship sessions with nothing written. I didn't think I had anything important to say, and even if I did, I had no clue where to begin. I had the voices of other people in my mind, who told me that I was too young to write a book . . . and I believed them. Who would want to read what I have to say?

At first, I felt more comfortable talking about everything but my own story. So I wrote all of these abstract ideas about my perspective on the universe and the world as I saw it, making sure to never mention anything about my journey, who I am, and where I've been. I left out that I am a queer woman of color, a first-generation Muslim American who came of age in the middle of Las Vegas, Nevada. I was worried about what my haters would think about me, people who would critique what I had to say and ridicule me for it. But those are not my people. Those are not the audience that I care about nor the ones that I am meant to serve. The people that I really want to speak to, that I can help, are people who share a similar journey to me in one way or another. People who see themselves in aspects of my story. Those who don't get spoken to enough in this world. It took me too long to affirm for myself how important my contributions are and that I, and people like me, deserve to take up space and be heard.

Now I know that I can always find myself through the process of creation. Through my paintings, my music, and my writing I discover who I truly am and what I deeply desire. No editor, no expert, no ghost-writer could write this book for me. No art teacher could paint it for me. I needed to sit down and find it within myself. I needed all of the strug-gle, all of the misery at the blank canvas or page, struggling to make my mark and let it out, to be where I am now. I needed to be in my messy, perfectly imperfect process, to cry on these pages and let my sacred creative wound out into the sun to breathe.

My whole life, I ran from doing this healing work in my creative practice. It wasn't that I was too busy; I was resistant to what I would find when I sat down with myself and the proverbial blank canvas of my life. All I wanted was intimacy. With myself as an artist and true connection with the people I admired and loved. But I was also afraid of that depth.

So I ran, until my Creative Mission showed that the only way to satiate the longing that I felt was to create an environment in which I felt safe to explore and express who I am. And I've had to find that sense of devotion, to show up day after day, until my art finally did create me. And it is all the love, intention, and healing energy that I find through my creative process that makes it sacred and divine. It's all the depth and beauty of being human that I see when I look at a finished canvas or as I finally hold this book in my hands. That's what I'm proud of: I'm making the creative and colorful art that my younger self was searching for.

The practice of sharing who I am in the moment is what's allowed me to love myself and find my voice. It's how I've integrated all of those parts that used to make me feel othered and instead found a sense of wholeness. This is how I heal myself in real time, and as soon as I unleash it into the world, I'm reminded that I'm not alone and actually I'm inextricably connected to a beautiful movement that's happening on this planet. And I don't have to be perfect, or the world's most talented artist, to make a difference in the lives of others and help them heal too. And it was that beautiful feedback that I needed to keep sharing no matter how uncomfortable it was. The moment I shared my truth in the world, even if it's messy, and let people into my healing journey because I knew that it was important, was the moment I found freedom.

Most of my work today is about pulling back the curtain and letting people into my process. I love being multidimensional and multifaceted. I honor my humanity and the areas that I'm still healing and growing in. It's so liberating to know that I don't have to put on a facade of perfection or having it all together. I'd rather be real. I'd rather be a walking permission slip. I'd rather be honest. Now, when I make art, I make it for me. I don't have to wonder what anyone else will think of it. I'm devoted to creating something that's healing. To leave my mark, a vibration that colorfully ripples out and transforms everything it touches.

Expansion Exercise

INNER CHILD HEALING

Sometimes difficult emotions can arise that have nothing to do with your current circumstances but instead stem from your sacred creative wound—which more often than not was created during your youth. When you find yourself emotionally overwhelmed, one of the best things you can do to calm your nervous system is to reparent yourself. Chances are, you've stuffed these emotions down for a long time because they're too painful to process. Or you might subconsciously seek approval, validation, or care for your inner child from an external source, like a romantic relationship. This never works. The truth is these emotions will continue to show up over and over again until you heal them and give yourself the love that you seek.

This exercise will help you get in touch with your emotions and locate them to your somatic body. Create a sacred space to do this inner child work by lighting a candle, calling on your spirit team, and setting an intention beforehand.

1. Consider your sacred creative wound. Is there a moment from your youth or childhood that has always weighed heavy on you, which may be the source of where this wound comes from? Let yourself go back to this place, and if it feels comfortable to you, give yourself permission to feel the honest emotions that it brings up.

2. Notice what you are feeling in your body. Where do you feel it? Scan your body to find where your emotions are showing up.

3. Sit quietly and self-observe. What does it feel like? Perhaps it's a tightness, a tingling, a closing, or an emptiness. Can you find words to describe how it feels? How might that relate to what you are currently healing in your sacred creative wound?

4. Tend to your body and emotions with gentleness and care. Ask this part of your body what it needs or wants to feel cared for. Listen deeply and see if you hear a response.

5. Once you get a response for what your sacred creative wound needs to feel nurtured and held, give yourself that. How can you quell the negative reactivity by reparenting yourself to avoid recurring patterns? If you let yourself feel and nurture it, you will begin to heal and liberate yourself from patterns that are no longer serving you.

Teaching

HEALING YOURSELF THROUGH YOUR CREATIVITY

All of us have something to heal. Some of us have a little more than others. And that's okay! When you actively engage in your own healing process, it's a win, not just for yourself, but for the entire collective. It benefits everyone in your life, as well as the entire world. The planet is literally on fire, and it's up to us to do something about it. When you nurture and restore yourself, you shift the consciousness of the planet toward a vibration of healing and self-love, which will positively affect everything in the universe starting with yourself. And if you're going to step into your Creative Mission as the badass Radiant Wildheart that you are, you will definitely need to lovingly tend to your wounds.

If you're an intuitive, empathic person, you're probably acutely aware of the things that need healing in your life. Never feel ashamed of that. There is nothing wrong with owning your own inner restoration project. In fact, it's something to be proud of.

So many people go through life half-asleep, incapable, or unwilling to self-reflect. As a result, they can cause harm to the people in their lives, often without even realizing it. You probably know someone in your life who refuses to heal and work on their own stuff. And you know how painful that can be for the people around them. The more you set your intentions toward holding a sacred space for yourself, the more you'll be able to be of service to others with all the gorgeous gifts you're cultivating.

If you're someone who feels like you have a lot of healing to do, I commend you for being honest with yourself. If you've lived a challenging life or feel intense emotions, your creativity is the perfect place to channel that energy. And those intense emotions often come with the territory of being someone as wildly magical as you are. So set the intention right now that from this point forward, you are here to heal and understand yourself.

Use your intuition to learn how to be your own Healer. You don't need to give your power away to others who claim they know what's best for you. The most powerful healers known are facilitators that help others restore themselves. Think of your creativity as the ultimate self-healer. Let it direct you and tell you what you need to heal yourself. Your creative spirit will speak to you and tell you what they need. Now is the time to give your sacred creative wound your devoted attention, to set the intention for self-healing and liberation, so that you no longer hold yourself back.

❦❧ CREATIVE PRACTICE ☙❧
Creative Healing

Creativity can transmute pain into something beautiful. For this creative practice, I'm asking you to spend time making a piece of art about something that you are currently healing. Choose a medium that resonates with you. I choose different mediums every day. You can create any kind of art you want: a scrapbook, a freestyle poem with the prompt, a floral arrangement, an altar in your home, a collage, a witchy ritual that you make up, a healing photoshoot, or anything else you might be inspired to do. The choice is yours. Let this be an open-ended assignment that is fully guided by the wisdom of your Intuitive Higher Self.

1. Choose a topic that you are currently healing and working through.

2. Sit quietly and reflect on this topic. Allow the medium and concept to emerge. Let it choose you and say yes once it feels right.

3. *Optional* Spend some time doing stream-of-consciousness writing about this topic beforehand to help you explore themes.

4. Start your art piece. Have fun with this process and keep your healing at the forefront throughout this journey. Let it be intuitively created, and don't have much or any of a plan. Let yourself be surprised by what comes through. You may find that you're expressing yourself honestly about this topic for the first time, speaking your truth about what happened and reframing it. Allow yourself even more permission to share authentically, knowing that no one else ever needs to see this but you. Let it take as long as you need: 10 minutes, a few hours, several days. Keep working on it until you feel complete.

5. Look at your work of art and reflect on what you learned during this process. What emotions shifted for you as you created it? How do you feel now that you've reached this point? How have you changed or transmuted on this healing journey?

BRAVERY

Sharing your art requires bravery. It takes profound courage to stand in your truth and be seen in it. Sure, being seen in your creativity might make you feel a little vulnerable at first. Fear and resistance can consume all of your energy. The antidote to this fear is to remember how freaking powerful you are! You are stronger and more capable than you realize, and with enough practice, you'll realize how many gifts come from cultivating that courage—feeling the fear but taking action anyway. Let yourself be motivated by something deeper, by the movement of your Creative Mission and finding those who are walking a similar path as you. And when you do, you'll realize that it was easier than you thought. And, more often than not, I see that when my students finally do share their work, they find it to be a lot more fun than they were expecting.

There may be people who don't respond well to your vulnerable shares. There are times when my own creative ideas flop. I've been criticized, made huge mistakes, or put something out that I was really excited about and . . . crickets. The reality is, some people won't be into what you do, and that's okay. You don't have to be for everybody, and you shouldn't want to be, anyway.

People who try to be for everyone wind up reaching no one. And if you're trying to bend into a pretzel to please everyone, you won't be sharing authentically or standing for what you believe. You'll end up attracting the wrong people into your life, and the misalignment will have a negative effect on your Creative Mission. If some people don't resonate with what you share, and you have no idea why, that's fine. It really isn't any of your business. The more you share your truth authentically, the more you'll find your people who celebrate the real you.

*"You can be the ripest, juiciest peach in the world,
and there's still going to be somebody who hates peaches."*

— Dita Von Teese

Expansion Exercise

3-STEP PRACTICE TO SHARE AND BE SEEN

It's healing to be seen in your creative expressions. Not just for you, but also for those who are blessed to come into contact with your creations as well. In this chapter, you've learned exactly how magical it can be to transmute your pain into a beautiful work of art. You can transmute and transform anything using your creativity as a healing modality if you set healing as your intention during your creative practice.

Now let's take it a step further. Your creations can heal you, but they also will change and transform those who get to experience them. The energy you put into your creation when you made it will be what people feel when they experience it. However, it will also bring up unique ideas that are specific to the prior knowledge and experience of the viewer. Regardless, when you are seen in your creativity, others can tap into your healing frequency through your work. Just by being willing to share your path from wound to recovery, by sharing your art, you are helping and in service to others. You don't have to do anything more than that to make a positive impact on this planet.

This simple, three-step process guides you through how your creativity can heal yourself and others if you allow yourself to both share and be witnessed.

STEP 1: **Make Art** If you want to create with the intention of healing, simply use your creative practices to explore a topic that feels alive for you right now. As an art educator, I loved giving art assignments and prompts to my students. But you can give yourself prompts and topics to explore. Start by asking yourself, What am I working through? Take a moment to openly examine what is coming up that needs your attention. Then use one of your creative practices to explore the topic without judgment. Replace that judgment with an open heart and childlike curiosity. Eventually, you'll get to a place where you can release shame and integrate those parts of yourself that are asking to be healed.

There's no right or wrong way to heal yourself through your art. If you feel an emotion coming up, let your Intuitive Higher Self be your guide, and turn that emotion into art. You may choose to continue working on the artwork you created earlier in this chapter, or you might decide to start something new. The choice is yours.

STEP 2: **Share with a Trusted Friend** Now it's time to share. Throughout this book, I have been letting you know that you can keep all of your creations to yourself so that it feels safer and more comfortable to explore. However, there is real medicine in letting yourself be seen in your creativity. So I want to invite you to invite someone else into your creative process. This can be a trusted individual, someone who you know will provide a safe, loving, and supportive space for you to share your precious creative baby. Perhaps let them know in advance that you aren't looking for criticism or feedback, but simply for witnessing and celebration.

Share in any way that feels comfortable for you. No share is too big or too small. Let yourself be vulnerable, perhaps naming that this is a sacred moment that is bringing up some nervous excitedness in you. The more you share, the more your confidence will grow. Eventually, you'll be able to expand to bigger audiences with a lot more ease. Or you might be bold enough to share it online or with a large group of people right away. That's wonderful too. But if that feels too scary, find a way that feels safe and comfortable for you. Keep it small and intimate. Sharing with just one person is enough to successfully complete this assignment.

STEP 3: **Be Witnessed** Once you've shared, I want you to intentionally notice the shift of energy that occurs. There's a profound transformational moment when someone sees you in your creativity. That transformation happens not just for you, but also for your witness. First, notice any differences that you feel after sharing your creation. How does it feel to be seen? Is it healing in any way?

Then I want you to receive any reflections or affirmations that your viewer may have. Do you notice anything shift in them? In your relationship?

The more that you share your work, the more you will notice that your creations have a tangible impact on people. This process is the first step in beginning to slow down and truly receive these moments as they happen, which will eventually give you a lot more confidence. Feeling seen is an important part of the healing process. But, in order to be seen, you have to be willing to put yourself out there first! I hope this was a safe and comfortable way for you to begin to be seen in your authentic expression.

INNER OVERPROTECTOR
The Impostor

Time to meet your next Inner Overprotector: The Impostor. The Impostor is very focused on what other people think of you. They are afraid that if you take up space and are seen, other people might find out you're not who you say you are. The Impostor keeps you from checking in with yourself or going inward to create as a way of healing yourself. When the Impostor is running the show, you can't focus on those deep inner emotions because you are too focused on what everyone else might think. This is counterproductive because it's impossible to make anything that feels authentic to you if you are constantly judging yourself and wondering if others will deem your work worthy or valuable.

You might be experiencing the Impostor if:

- You rely on other people's opinions about your creative work in order to move forward.

- You feel incapable or inadequate on your own and are always wondering what's missing.

- You don't stop to check in with your own healing journey and how it relates to your creative process.

- You are afraid to speak your truth, take up space, and be seen for fear of being found out.

- You don't think your original ideas are good enough so you compare yourself to others.

Tips for Dealing with the Impostor:

- Create something with the intention that no one will ever see it but you. As you create, ask yourself, *What would feel healing for me in this moment?* and then do that.

- Spend time journaling about the root of your fears. What are you actually afraid of? What's the worst thing that would happen if someone does reject you?

- Remind yourself that you don't have to be for everyone. In fact, to lead a world-changing Creative Mission, you really only need to find a handful of truly aligned souls. In order to find those people who are really aligned, it's important that you lead with your authenticity. When people identify themselves as not being a fit for your work, that's a win for you because you don't want misaligned people in your energetic field anyway!

Healing is not linear

HEALING IS A SPIRAL

You don't have to be fully healed to be of service to others. Healing is not linear. Many people keep pursuing self-improvement thinking they'll reach a final destination of wholeness. But the reality is that no one is fully healed.

Some people get so stuck in the process that it becomes an excuse to isolate. Can you accept yourself as you are right now in your process? You don't always have to strive to change yourself. You don't always have to be doing the work. Sometimes it's best to accept yourself exactly where you are.

Healing is a positive spiral. You'll continuously circle back to revisit the same wounds, but in different cycles of your life and from a more evolved place. You might think you've healed something and then a few years later, it will pop up again with a familiar emotion that you thought you had already worked through. That doesn't mean you're back at square one. It just means you're on a different part of the spiral, with a different view, having gained more wisdom and information to address it in a new way.

Sharing your healing journey with others can help you pass through the winding turns of the spiral, so you don't have to do it alone. This act of sharing with people you trust can facilitate your healing, because sometimes these wounds just want to be expressed and moved. When you share, you also have the added benefit of empowering someone else to learn a bit more about themselves. Your people will see themselves in your journey, and that in and of itself can be so healing.

Archetype Spotlight

THE ELEMENTAL APPROACH TO SELF-HEALING

 MYSTIC—Tap into your spirit team and have them do the heavy lifting for deeper healing jobs. You have this incredible, ethereal resource; don't forget to use it and *ask* for their help! When you call upon your guardian angels, healed ancestors, ascended masters, muses, plant allies, and animal spirits, you can ask them to assist you on your healing journey. Remember that you are never alone. Your spirit team can help you to heal yourself.

 VISIONARY—You are so focused on healing the collective, but you need to remember that healing yourself *is* going to help the collective. Because of your airy-fairy nature, you have a tendency to be focused outwardly, buzzing around and connecting with people and ideas. This is wonderful, and we love your ability to hold the bigger picture for your community. But in order to live your Creative Mission in a sustainable way, you need to focus your healing efforts on yourself first! Without you, there is no Creative Mission or service. And we need you and your vision. So remember, your projects will go so much further when you tend to your own personal healing, and that will ripple out to positively impact those in your life.

 SACRED REBEL—By nature, you are very comfortable in the fires of transformation. This can often be an intense process, and there is lots of healing that happens as you alchemize your experiences into something new. You might find that you are constantly being reborn and rising from the ashes of old stories that no longer serve you. How comfortable are you with these phases of change, transformation, and growth in your life?

Can you welcome healing in, knowing that this is part of your unique genius for how you serve in the world? Also, don't be afraid to lighten up a bit. While your healing journey is deep, it doesn't have to be so serious all the time! That lightness will make the process of transformation so much more fun.

 HEALER—Healing is your thing! As a watery-being, you are here not just to heal yourself but to be a beacon of inspiration for others to step into their own healing gifts and frequency. That's why we call you the Healer! You do this simply by showing up and being who you are. Your natural way of being is to heal through your beautiful sensitivity and hold the space for others to slow down and be with their emotions. Your energy reminds people that they want to heal for themselves and for the collective. This is your gift, so lean in to it. These complex emotions that you notice are what make us so beautifully human. Embrace the complexities and let them inspire you with their profound depth. That way, you won't feel overwhelmed by the endless healing journey you experience while you live your Creative Mission.

 GUARDIAN—Your grounded and steadfast presence is inspiring to others and allows them to feel safe. You might be hard on yourself, but it's because you have extremely high standards for the quality of your work. Try to relax because you naturally emit a healing energy that people love to be around. The space that you hold naturally is one that allows people to feel emotionally held and come back down to earth.

PART IV

Living Your
Creative Mission

Wildheart, you've been on such a magical journey. I want to honor how far you've come. You've reclaimed your inner artist. You've taken the time and space to cultivate your creative practices, and you've liberated your Radiant Wildheart self. Now it's time for you to take all of the work you've been doing on yourself and put it into service to the world. Your Creative Mission is where your impact and creativity meet. We do all of this inner work not just for our own liberation, but so we can advance our Creative Mission. This is the moment when your training wheels come off.

＊

लोकाः समस्ताः सुखिनो भवन्तु

May all beings everywhere be happy and free, and may the thoughts, words, and actions of my own life contribute in some way to that happiness and that freedom for all.

— LOKAH SAMASTAH SUKHINO BHAVANTU

If you look around, you'll see how needed you are in this world. Extreme weather due to climate change is impacting all of humanity. Politically, we are extremely divided. And so many people are stifled under oppression and hatred. If you have the privilege to be able to help others liberate themselves, you must. No one has the luxury to wait around. Now is the time to step into service and leadership. The revolution is here, and you have an essential role to play in it.

With all of the passionate, creative energy you've been cultivating, you have the power to uplift your community in a way that will benefit our entire planet. In a way that only you can. When our Earth suffers, we all feel its pain. But so many of us have become numb to this ache due to colonization and globalization. Those of us with marginalized identities can't escape the reality that we are literally fighting for our lives. But for some, it's easier to turn a blind eye. To be a Radiant Wildheart in this world means to also be a part of a bigger change that's happening. We must not bypass this pain. We must lean in to it and use it to inspire action within ourselves. It's time for you to create your unique path forward so that you can do your part to heal yourself, your communities, and the planet.

And you don't have to sacrifice your authentic self to do it. Your revolution will be filled with love, nourishment, and self-care. It will be wildly creative, colorful, and as unique as you are. And you, as a Radiant Wildheart, will make your impact, not by grinding and hustling, but by becoming fully embodied in your truth. Eventually, with enough practice, this kind of inclusive leadership will become second nature to you. And you won't need to think so hard about what to do next because your Creative Mission will guide you to exactly where you need to be.

In this section, you will step powerfully into your Creative Mission as a fully embodied Radiant Wildheart. The first chapter of this section is all about leadership. Developing strong leadership skills is vital for you to spark your movement. From there, you're going to learn the ins and outs of community building. You'll learn to foster a nurturing community that supports you and vice versa. And finally, our last chapter is about embodiment. It's about living your creativity in every area of your life so you can create the changes that our planet so desperately needs just by being who you are.

Whether you are impacting the lives of a few people, or many, you can make a difference. Even if you reach only one other person, all of this will be worth it. Your Creative Mission can look however you want, so long as you contribute in your own unique way. This is the Creative Mission that your soul accepted when you incarnated on this planet. And all of the work we have been doing up until now has been giving you the strength and confidence you need to walk your talk and embody the dream you've envisioned for our world.

Remember, the universe wants to support this work. Your entire spirit team is rallying behind you to help you fulfill your Creative Mission. Without you, an essential piece of the puzzle is missing. So, if there's any part of you that is still holding you back, release it now. Holding on to these fears is counterproductive. You are embraced by the divine. Your presence is a gift and is urgently requested in this fight for the sustainability and healing of our planet.

CHAPTER TEN

Leadership

Lead from the Heart to Change the World

I never used to see myself as a leader. I was more of an observer. During important conversations, I would sit in the back like a wallflower, doodling in my notebook instead of contributing. And when I did have something to say, my throat would tighten and my chest would contract. Online, when I wanted to share my opinions on important issues, I would post but then immediately delete it before anyone could see it. I second-guessed and judged myself, fearing that whatever I said would be wrong.

It was easier to feign disinterest and act like I didn't care than to admit I would be hurt by rejection. I rarely felt that true connection and intimacy with others, where I felt seen and acknowledged, and I wanted that. But I had gotten so used to hiding my true self from the world. I told myself that I was just different, a rebel without a cause that nobody understood. I pretended that I would rather just party and have fun than build intimate relationships with others . . . or with myself. But in reality, I was numbing myself.

My favorite coping mechanism was to keep myself safe by staying emotionally isolated. I put up lots of walls and subconsciously refused to connect deeply with anyone. Because if no one could get close to me, no one could hurt me. I prided myself on marching to the beat of my own drum. I filled my plate up with work and creative projects so that I was too busy to get close to others. I learned how to rely on no one but myself. It just felt easier on my own. And safer too.

Lead from the Heart, to Change the World

I ran away from real connections, intimacy, my emotions—anything that made me vulnerable. Because if people saw the real me, and rejected me, then what would that mean? This avoidance led to a chain of broken agreements with anyone who tried to get close to me. I wouldn't return their calls. I'd show up late for meetings. I was unreliable. If people tried to get too close, I would find a way to push them away. I was a proud lone wolf, leaving it up to the "leader types" to make decisions and doing my own thing in the meantime.

I was the author of my own tragedy. I would find myself in the same situations with different people, over and over again. I would spiral, wondering if those I cared about were upset with me for one reason or another. I let the wrong people into my life: ones who didn't recognize or honor my worth. I felt guilty when I put up a boundary. I constantly fell into unhealthy situations, overwhelming drama, and chaotic relationships.

People thought that I was aloof, but that couldn't have been further from the truth. In reality, there was nothing that I wanted more than to be recognized for my gifts. I'd been hungry for that recognition since I was a little girl. I never let people see me cry, but underneath the surface, there were a storm of emotions.

When I lived my life this way, I kept perpetuating the story that I was unlovable or unworthy. But eventually my patterns of self-sabotage became impossible to ignore.

I decided to take on myself as a creative project. I did the deep work to tend to my inner child, a little girl who was longing to be seen. As I did, I started to heal. The more I healed, the more I connected to that pain I'd been numbing. And the more I learned to love myself, the more I realized how much I do care about the world around me.

I'm still on a journey of peeling back the layers that had kept me hiding and in emotional isolation. I suspect that this will be a lifelong process of recognizing and understanding what beauty I bring to the world. But the more I let people in and allow my creativity to be a deep act of service, the bigger the impact I seem to make. The more I stop numbing myself, and let myself feel everything, even the pain that I once tried to numb, the more I realize how important it is to feel connected. Our state of disconnection from ourselves and from what's happening on our planet is getting us nowhere fast. But when you allow yourself to acknowledge the longing you feel for something better, for change, it's natural to want to do something about it. Your creativity then can be offered as an act of service. It's the gift that you give to the world that makes a tangible impact in more places than you'll ever be able to realize.

You might not be a perfect leader yet, and you don't have to be. The real magic is in showing up, even if you don't know what you're doing, and declaring that you want to use your time on this planet to create a positive change. You can change the world just by being yourself. And by living your Creative Mission, your life becomes a deep act of service, a love letter to the planet and all of its inhabitants. A reimagining of the world the way that you want to see it.

❤❯❯❯❯ CREATIVE PRACTICE ❮❮❮❮❤
Abundance Journal Prompt

There are lots of different ways to be a leader, and there's space for all different types of people to rise up and serve. Take some time to journal about the following prompts to help you better understand the styles of leadership that resonate with you. Remember that when you can see positive qualities in other people, it's because you carry those qualities too. You might not be able to see it yet, but it's true. Journal about the following questions to learn more about your authentic leadership style.

- Who are the people who stick out in your mind as great leaders? What qualities do they have?

- Which leaders do not resonate with you? What qualities do they have?

- Where are you already showing up as a leader? Where do you *aspire* to lead?

You are a unique being, and you get to find your own style as a leader. This will involve finding the balance of maintaining your individuality while still being committed to the transformation of others. Stepping more deeply into your leadership will be a wonderful practice in bettering your communication skills and strengthening your boundaries. This will keep you feeling safe and honored as you stretch into new levels of service in the world.

Teaching

FOUR PRINCIPLES OF LEADERSHIP

Your life is your prayer to humanity, and leadership is an expression of your love. I am so grateful for all I've learned about what makes an effective and empowering leader. Leadership is a skill that is developed over time. It's the number one skill that's allowed me to live my Creative Mission, make an impact, and even get paid for my contributions to the world. Being able to support others in their process of becoming has made my life rich with meaning. No matter the difficult experiences you find yourself moving through, your leadership and service to the world will allow you to sleep soundly at night, knowing that you are making a real difference. And that's something no one can ever take away from you.

I know you are longing to live a life of purpose. You are here because you want to experience something more profound than just going through the motions of business as usual. You want to empower yourself while empowering others. Your ability to hone your leadership skills will allow you to make shifts happen for you and for others at a much faster rate. Whether you want to start a creative project, a sacred business, a book club, or an affinity group, leadership skills will give you what you need to create it.

Here are some principles of leadership that I use to step into service in an empowered and energetically aligned way.

1. Live with integrity

Influential leaders live with integrity. For you to trust yourself and others to trust you, you must be someone who keeps your word. If you are constantly breaking promises to yourself, you're sending the message to your subconscious that you are unreliable. And if that's how you feel, chances are, you will not see yourself as an effective leader and will hold yourself back from opportunities because of it.

I love the motto, "How you do one thing is how you do everything." Because if you are constantly breaking promises to yourself, you are probably doing the same thing to other people in your life. If you notice that you continuously make agreements that you don't keep, you may want to journal and meditate on the word *integrity* and what it means to you.

If you feel that you have work to do in this area, don't worry. I did too. But my life improved dramatically once I started living in integrity with my values. This meant showing up for my loved ones more often, speaking up for what I believed in, and removing myself from situations that no longer aligned with who I wanted to be.

When you started this book, you set an intention for your creativity and self-expression. Now that you are ready to take your creativity out into the world, it helps to add another layer to that intention. What's your intention for living your Creative Mission? Why do you want to step into service and connect your life to a movement that's bigger than yourself? If you can remember why you are stepping into service, it becomes a lot easier to act in accordance with your integrity.

As creatives, I believe that we need accountability. You need to hold yourself accountable, and as a leader, you're also going to be holding others accountable. Similarly, those under your leadership will also be expecting a level of integrity, transparency, and authenticity from you. Having clear agreements with others allows you to serve in a way that feels good for you. You can always renegotiate an agreement that you made in a way that honors all parties, if necessary. Make sure that you practice integrity by speaking up with clear communication in advance. Be transparent. Allow yourself to be human and make mistakes. Be honest. This prevents negative feelings on all sides and helps you manage people's expectations. You don't have to be perfect, but you do get to be authentic. And that goes a long way in leadership.

2. Speak your truth

It can feel scary to take a stand for your beliefs. It can even feel unsafe. But here's the thing: you need to lead with your values. Because not leading with your values, your ethics, your beliefs, and what you stand for will keep you separated from your Creative Mission.

Leaders say what they are thinking. If you are going to make an impact, you must stand up for your beliefs. Of course, pick your battles. I am not recommending you confront every single injustice you see or be deliberately contrary or inflammatory or provocative, especially if that goes against your most authentic nature. However, you do need to speak your mind and get off the sidelines.

For me, leading with my values means committing to my own personal decolonization. I used to be afraid to speak up for what I believed in for fear it would be polarizing. But now, I'm committed to living with integrity and don't need to be liked by everyone. If you're finding that you have a hard time speaking your truth, I encourage you to find people who are aligned with your values that you can hang out around. When you have a values-aligned community, it's a lot easier to feel safe to practice sharing your opinions and being seen in your truth. And it shows you that you are not alone in your beliefs, identities, and experiences, which is so healing.

Ultimately, living in your truth and being an advocate for yourself and others feels powerful AF. Our liberation is inherently bound up together. When those who are the most oppressed get free, we all do too. So it's up to you to be brave. If you see something that needs to be changed, change it. And don't be afraid to advocate for yourself and those around you that you care about. We need your voice. If you feel afraid, find others to stand with you and support you! You don't have to do this alone. Your community is here for you.

Your truth could be revolutionary and profoundly healing for someone out there who has a similar journey as you, and these are the people who are going to want to work with you. Yes, you have to get brave. Yes, you have to take that risk. Yes, your voice can create change in the world.

3. Learn healthy boundaries

Having healthy boundaries creates the space for you to be limitless because they allow you to feel safe and respected. When you have healthy boundaries, everybody wins. You'll be able to show up at your fullest capacity knowing that you not only feel supported by others but also by yourself. Boundaries allow you to protect your energy and fill your cup so you can give from the overflow. You deserve to protect your peace of mind. You deserve to preserve your mental and physical well-being by creating healthy boundaries that give you the space you need to thrive.

Boundaries show up in all relationships: romantic, professional, family, and friendships. Without healthy boundaries, you might find yourself being pushed around by the needs, wants, and desires of others. And when you don't have healthy boundaries, you sacrifice your identity and individuality. I believe that having healthy boundaries is crucial for everybody on this planet. Because if everyone takes care of their own needs first, all of our relationships would be so much healthier and abundant.

Sometimes boundaries can be hard for others to respect because our society teaches that we aren't supposed to have them. But if something doesn't feel good for you, you are at liberty to create the boundaries that allow you to recalibrate back to your own centered energy. You don't need to feel guilty for expressing your boundaries and reinforcing them. Some people may take your boundaries as an attack, but that's their problem, not yours. And usually the people who are upset by your boundaries are those who benefited from you not having any.

While I do think discovering and naming your boundaries in a clear yet gentle way is a practice, so is tuning in to your inner wisdom to find out when something isn't sitting right with you. If you feel bothered or upset and are unsure why, it's likely that a boundary of yours is being unknowingly crossed. If you are someone who isn't used to setting healthy boundaries for yourself, find and cherish those who honor your boundaries and check with you about them. Those are the people who will allow you to live with enough space for your true nature to flourish.

If you plan to step into leadership, healthy boundaries with yourself and others are essential. Boundaries with yourself could look like making sure you're not filling every single moment of free space with new commitments and agreements that keep you from being fully present with your service. Your healthy boundaries will allow you to create a safe and secure container that others feel held within. This is especially important if you are holding space for another person's healing or transformation journey.

When you proactively set boundaries, you protect your energy and psyche, so you don't carry other people's trauma and emotional work home with you. The people you serve will feel supported by the crystal clear energy exchange between you and them. And your Creative Mission will feel a lot more sustainable for you in the long term.

4. Listen to feedback

One of the things I'm most proud of as a leader is my ability to listen to feedback and make changes accordingly. Life is always giving you feedback. If you look around at your environment right now, you'll probably get an idea of how things are going. The feedback you get doesn't need to be deemed good or bad. It's just information. The way to refine your leadership is by listening to the feedback that you're receiving all around you. When I notice patterns of energy leaks, boundary issues, unhappy clients, or my own people-pleasing, I take it as useful data, and I make changes accordingly.

Sometimes it can be challenging to take an honest look at the feedback you're getting. It's easy to get into our egos and feel like we're being criticized or judged. I know how hard it can be because you're an intuitive, heart-centered, and emotional being who is deeply connected to your work. When your creative expression feels so personal, it's tempting to get all up in your feelings when you receive feedback that doesn't feel positive. But if you can put your ego aside and see feedback as the gift that it is, you'll create powerful shifts that align you with your purpose.

The truth is, living your Creative Mission is a continuous process of tweaking and testing to find what works best. There is no neat and tidy path to your full self-expression. Making revisions is an important part of the creative process. Instead of looking at a situation to see what's wrong with you (because nothing is, I promise you're awesome!), look at what could be improved and find the bits of information hiding in there. The feedback that's being offered to you is a gift. It's happening *for* you and in service to your liberation.

Stay curious and ask yourself the following questions:

+ *What could be done better next time?*

+ *What could I tweak and experiment with?*

+ *How can I make the experience feel more aligned with my values?*

+ *How could I make this feel simpler, easier, and more fun?*

The best thing that you can do is get out there and do the dang thing, completely aware that you will probably have to course correct. You're going to be growing and changing every day, and that's a great thing. With each day, you're going to become a stronger and more aligned leader if you are willing to self-reflect. I invite you to examine this constant feedback loop you're receiving from your life, from your leadership, from your results, and ask yourself: *What is the information being presented to me here?*

Let that information be the gift that guides you to your next aligned step.

INNER OVERPROTECTOR
The Wallflower

It's time to meet your next Inner Overprotector, the Wallflower. The Wallflower doesn't speak up because they don't want to be judged. The Wallflower sits in the back of the room, letting everyone else take the lead. They do this, not because they want to evade responsibility, but because they're unsure if you'll do it right and they want to protect you from being cast out or ridiculed. The Wallflower may pretend not to care about being a part of the team. They worry about what might happen if you stand out rather than stay silent and blend into the crowd. There's a risk in standing out! You could be rejected, or worse!

Over time, that lack of action will make you feel disempowered and hopeless, telling you to tune out your desires to have an impact or express your differences proudly, because you are not powerful enough to do anything about it, anyway. So why bother? But change is possible, and you are capable of creating it if you're willing to take the risk and be seen in your truth.

You may be experiencing the Wallflower if:

+ You sit in the back of the classroom or conference room instinctively.

+ You feel that other people are better leaders than you, so you wait for someone else to take the lead before offering your opinion.

+ You tend to blend into the crowd. When you're in classes or workshops, people might not remember you or know you were there.

+ You feel like being a part of most teams is pointless and doubt that you or anyone can make much of a difference at all.

Tips for Dealing with the Wallflower:

+ Find safe spaces where you can practice being seen. Try raising your hand and asking a question every once in a while or sharing something about yourself in one of the groups or programs that you are in.

+ Have a "brilliant bragging" practice with a friend or accountability buddy of yours. Call each other up once a week to celebrate and revel in the juicy parts of your life that you're excited about, big or small.

+ Find a small and easy way to step into leadership. Perhaps you start a book club or a meetup group, or you teach a class to one of your friends about something you're good at! Be creative and keep it simple just to flex those leadership muscles.

Expansion Exercise
WILDHEART MEETUP GROUP

Okay, Wildheart, it's time for you to step into leadership. Your task is to create your own Wildheart Meetup Group. This can be about anything you like. Think of it as an affinity group, which is any group that is formed around a shared interest. Your Wildheart Meetup could be as simple as a book club. Or it might be you convening with people who share a similar interest as you, whether it's music, entrepreneurship, healing, or anything else under the sun.

Facilitating anything makes you a leader. When you create your Wildheart Meetup Group, you're going to be making choices around the topic of the meeting, the dates, and the location; and you'll be communicating with your group to ensure that they show up. This in itself is a huge demonstration of leadership.

Don't overthink this assignment. Your Wildheart Meetup can be as big or small as you like. But if this is your first time putting together an event, let it be easy. Invite three to five people out for a meal and discuss a shared topic! Don't try and make this assignment such a large-scale production that you stall on making it happen.

If you can't think of anything, start a book club around a particular book you already love and see what comes of it. You have total permission to start a book club around this book, and to lead discussions with your group about the chapters and exercises herein. See what it feels like to have a discussion around these topics and how that might deepen your own understanding of the content provided here.

Your meetup can look any way you want. It could be a formal meetup that you post about online, or perhaps it's as simple as you and two of your friends meeting for dinner and a conversation. Prepare a couple of talking points in advance for you to discuss with your meetup group. And voilà! You're a leader!

WHEN IN DOUBT, JUST SHOW UP

You don't have to have all the answers right now in order to lead. You don't need to be the world's foremost expert or even reach total mastery in a subject in order to help somebody through it. You just need to be a few steps ahead on the path. Right now, you might not feel like you have the confidence to actually make a difference. But the more you wait to feel ready, the more resistance you'll create within yourself. The feelings of readiness and confidence come from choosing to show up and lead over and over again. If you keep showing up consistently and continue to strengthen your visibility muscle, one day you'll wake up and realize that you're not actually all that afraid of being seen anymore. Living your Creative Mission will feel like second nature to you.

Yes, it feels scary at first. That fear can be intense. But the most effective way to move through your resistance is to just go for it and see how you feel on the other side. I can tell you that 100 percent of the time, my clients feel amazing after they stretch themselves into being more visible. Even when you "mess up" (p.s. there's no such thing in my book!), even when you stutter or stumble or your mind goes blank, it's okay! Chances are, nobody will even register a little natural bump in the road when you're sharing authentically and passionately from your heart.

Let me tell you one more key secret. It's not about you. It's not about whether people like you. It's not about whether you say things in just the right way or your hair looks perfect. It's actually about the difference that you're making for other people. You have the opportunity to be the role model that you have always needed. But that's going to require you to be brave and get out of your own way.

Leadership means that you're willing to go first. You might need to be the first person to be vulnerable or make the first move. You might be the first person in your family to take these steps toward your liberation.

You'll have to let people into your process and be willing to show up as your perfectly imperfect self. And when you do, you'll create a ripple effect in the world that will allow other people to show up just as they are too.

You don't need to have it all figured out. All you have to do is be willing to uplift others and lead with your heart and your compassion. To be an effective leader, you must open up to see the humanity of others. Highlight their gifts and encourage them to find their own leadership skills. If you're in a leadership position, don't be the "boss," just telling people what to do. Instead, ask better questions. Help people find the answers for themselves. Facilitate their growth by holding them high and opening the door to possibility. And when all else fails, just show up.

Archetype Spotlight

FINDING YOUR STYLE OF LEADERSHIP

 MYSTIC—Ethereal beings can be long-winded, sharing lots of abstract ideas about consciousness and the multidimensional universe without ever saying anything about your personal story. You truly feel from another dimension, but the reality is that you were born on Earth for a reason. You have a unique and fascinating life story that you should give yourself the space to explore. When you speak from your own personal experience versus abstract concepts you've discovered in the ethereal realm, your message will feel a lot more grounded, and people will be able to understand what you're talking about.

 VISIONARY—Air beings are gifted at telling their story to influence the world and create change. And clear communication is an important aspect of being an effective leader. You love to chat, and because you're connected to your story, you talk with ease. But you have so many ideas with so much to say that sometimes you can dilute your message. Can you try to be more concise with your words? Practice telling your story, writing your story, and exploring it before you share. Try to speak with intention and say only what's necessary to make your impact much stronger. Your creative practice will show you what's important to help you spark your movement and inspire your people.

 SACRED REBEL—Most people see fire beings as being super confident, but I know that you don't always feel that way. You're great at speaking and sharing, but you might still find yourself doubting whether what you're sharing is important or worthy. But you don't have to be *on* all the time, and we all have moments where we aren't quite feeling our best. In fact, the most powerful and admirable leaders are the ones who can own their struggle and be authentic and vulnerable through it.

 HEALER—Oh, the drama of it all! As water beings, sometimes your emotions might land on other people as a bit theatrical even though you're feeling everything extra deep. It's a gift to be an emotionally connected and sensitive leader who makes other people feel seen, heard, and safe. However, just make sure you don't get stuck in your emotions for too long. Give yourself a certain amount of time to process, grieve, cry, or whatever. And then pick yourself back up and show up for your commitments to your Creative Mission.

 GUARDIAN—Earth beings have a deep desire to heal the planet. It's embedded into everything that you do. You're a humanitarian at heart, and you are grounded and can back it up. The world needs you to step into your leadership, but you need to be the one that gives yourself permission to take up space in that way. If you see something that needs to be done, be the one who takes action. Don't overthink it. People will be so appreciative of you and your earthy energy.

CHAPTER ELEVEN

Community

Nurture a Garden of Authentic Relationships

My chosen community is the reason I've survived. Even though I used to be a lone wolf, I needed to find a sense of belonging to live true to my Creative Mission. Intuitively, I've always known this. I felt disconnected at school and at home, but that doesn't mean I existed in a vacuum. I've always found a handful of people to connect deeply with, people with whom I could be my wild, uninhibited self and fill entire rooms with our cosmic laughter and joy. Now, I know that my best skills are in networking. I call them #ButterflySkills, because no matter where I am, I can always find someone that inspires me. Connecting with fellow Wildhearts and building together is how I've always understood the world and eventually how I found my purpose within it.

I will give you tips on how to build a **sacred support system** around yourself. Your sacred support system includes your chosen community but also extends much further. By the end of this chapter, you'll know how to intentionally create an environment around you that nourishes and supports you as you continue to live your Creative Mission and watch it ripple out into the world.

I started building my chosen community when I was 14, right around the time I began to embrace my inner Sacred Rebel. I knew I wasn't going to find many people to connect with at my bougie prep school, so I took to the Internet to find people with similar interests as me. As I started to make friends with other teens who loved music and art, I realized I could build meaningful connections online that didn't make me feel so alone (*disclaimer* always use your best discernment and intuition when connecting online with people you don't know). I made my first Internet friend when I was 14 from reading an online zine that I'd subscribed to (think of it like a super-early blog before they were popular). I received an e-mail from a girl my age in Salt Lake City named Angelica. I had never met her, but like me, she was an angsty, emo-pop-punk-loving teenager who was struggling with her home life and sharing her story online as a form of self-expression.

We need each other

Angelica would send messages out to her audience every day about her typical teenage life, filled with the usual things for alternative teens like us: music, deep feelings, crushes, and day-to-day activities. There were no pictures, just words. In one of her e-mails, she wrote that she was coming to Las Vegas to go to a concert that I also wanted to attend. It was my favorite band at the time, and it was hers too. The problem was,

I didn't have any actual friends to go with to the concert. I e-mailed her back, and we made plans to meet up.

We met in line at the concert and instantly became friends. I never told my parents about it because I knew they wouldn't be stoked about me meeting a stranger from the Internet. Luckily, Angelica was who she said she was, and we had a blast together. We belted our favorite lyrics while moshing with people who were much older than us. At the time, I hadn't met anyone like her. She was funny, unique, an authentic Aquarius who was more down to earth than anyone I knew. She made me feel comfortable, understood, and even cool. To this day, we are still friends.

We're both total Sacred Rebels in our own way, having grown into our values and unique identities in a way that continues to be complementary and supportive. While we might not talk all the time, we are constantly connected and in community because we both openly share our journey and evolution on social media and can celebrate each other from afar.

Meeting Angelica was the beginning of a long journey of finding and making connections with other lone wolves who didn't quite know where they belonged, but were willing to express themselves by sharing about their lives and letting the world in. In high school, when people would talk about being a part of a certain group, I prided myself on the fact that I floated in between all of them.

Over time, I got intentional about my desire to be around other artists. Even though I didn't consider myself an artist, I wanted to be around people who inspired me, who were open about their perspectives of the world, authentically shared their truth, and spoke up for what they believed in. I would stay out all night in the park with these artist friends of mine, talking about anything and everything that was going on in our lives and our perspective on our human experience. Without that chosen community, I don't know how I would have survived my teenage years.

As I got older and started coming to terms with my queerness, I knew I needed to be around people who understood. In college, I started to fully embrace parts of myself that previously made me feel confused and out of place. I attended a very progressive school, Smith College, with a predominantly queer population. I got to see all of the many ways to express and identify as a queer person, as someone who thinks, lives, and loves outside of any boxes. Being immersed in a queer community helped me embrace all the dynamic and sometimes even paradoxical aspects of my own identity. I could be all of myself at once. Queer, radical, creative, emotional, philosophical, intellectual, wild, poetic, and everything else that makes me who I am. And I found people who celebrated me for it.

My queer community has been a safe haven. People who understand what it was like to grow up being a bit of a misfit, different, and feeling like we needed to hide parts of ourselves. Because of that, we were able to liberate each other by celebrating the things that made us different. It was our diversity that made us so resilient, wise, and powerful. With their reflections and affirmations, long conversations into the night about all of our feelings on the state of the world, I realized the things that made me unique were revolutionary. A voice that needed to be heard. I'm so proud of my queer community! So many of my chosen family have gone on to lead world-changing Creative Missions. They've written amazing books, made beautiful music, and inspired policy changes because of the strength we've gained from lifting each other out of shame and into pride. It's a true celebration of what it means to be human.

After college, I moved back to Los Angeles, where I didn't know anyone. Once again, I spent time pouring my heart out online via my blog. One day, I was scrolling through my feed on Tumblr when I came across a post from a girl who casually mentioned that she was also a Bangladeshi queer femme living in Los Angeles. It's pretty rare to come across another queer South Asian person, and especially someone who is Bangladeshi, so I naturally reached out to her. She was so welcoming. I'm sure she too was used to finding and cultivating real community in these virtual spaces. She responded by inviting me to an event happening the following weekend hosted by Satrang—a queer, South Asian community that has existed in LA for decades—because, well, in a culture where our families of origin are often not accepting of this important aspect of our identity, we need each other.

My social anxiety kicked into high gear as I headed out somewhere in East LA. But when I walked up a set of cobblestone stairs, the familiar smell of Indian food filled the air. A ton of people wore Indian clothes. There was a gorgeous performance choreographed by Bollywood dancers, only this time, the performances were done by LGBTQ+ community members in drag.

I have been to lots of drag shows and countless Indian parties. But I had never seen the two merged together. And I had never been in a space where I could simultaneously be both South Asian and queer at the same time. I was used to hiding my queerness at these Indian functions, but here, I didn't have to. And I didn't know how to hold these two identities at once.

Most of the people I met were around my age, and afterward, we went to a classic Echo Park diner, the Brite Spot, for food. I sat next to a woman named Anjali who immediately felt like a big sister. I opened up to her about what I was experiencing, and she acknowledged how special it was that we could build queer kinship and family bonds since most of us didn't have that growing up. She ended up paying for my meal because, in our culture, the younger siblings never pay. It was such a touching gesture. It filled me with a feeling of belonging that I had been looking for my whole life.

My love for community and networking eventually spilled over into my career. As an elementary school art teacher, I emphasized the principles of a safe and respectful community to all my classes. This was essential in order for my students to explore their creativity and take risks with their artwork. Eventually, I realized that I wanted to pursue even more projects that would build community and healing through the arts, so I started my nonprofit, Green Seed Arts, that focused on collaborative creative projects.

By saying yes to my desire to form healing communities, I created unforgettable experiences that helped me find myself as a creative leader and facilitator. I worked with people who had just gotten out of prison. We made paintings about climate change and our reverence for the planet. I helped bring a beautiful mobile art studio to a music festival so that people could paint while watching their favorite artists perform. My goal was to show people that together we can create something more powerful and beautiful than we could on our own. And the metaphors and symbolisms for those projects are still teaching me how profound it is to put our creative hearts and hands together to make a tangible difference in the world.

Once I started my business and worked toward earning an income, it was easy to forget about these powerful experiences. I taught business and marketing, but the part of myself that facilitated creative experiences for community building was put on the back burner. In the process, I had stopped painting for a couple of years. I wasn't making as much art and was instead teaching my communities how to make money through their gifts. This is important, for sure. I still very much believe that we all deserve to get paid well to do what we love. But, making money isn't the point of your creativity.

I felt like something crucial was missing. I knew I needed to reunite with my creative side and merge it into my work with Radiant Wildhearts in order to feel fulfilled in my mission. I didn't know what it would look like. But I trusted that my creativity would show me the path forward.

At a business retreat, I shared my determination to reclaim my inner artist. I confessed that I had always wanted to lead an international community-building painting project, following in the footsteps of Lily Yeh, a mosaic artist who uses collaborative art projects to heal communities that have experienced the traumas of war and poverty. Before that retreat, I felt like I wasn't capable of leading an international painting project. I didn't think I was a good enough or legitimate enough artist to be able to pull it off. That was for professionals, and I still lacked the confidence to understand the kind of change I could bring . . . even though I had already been doing it for years!

My muses wouldn't let me forget about it though. And I knew that that fear meant there was something very important for me held in that dream that I told myself wasn't possible. And in order to reclaim my inner artist, I had to pick that dream up off the shelf and make it a reality.

To my surprise, I found the exact support I needed to make it happen right there within that community. Once I admitted my dream aloud, a friend of mine approached me. Her name is Sherina, and she's a beautiful Healer and coach with a heart of service. Something about my creative dream spoke to her, and she said, "Whatever you need to make it happen, I've got you."

With her support, we were able to get a project supporting teenage mothers living in poverty fully funded by our communities. We found a team of people who aligned with our values and wanted to give back too. We led a phenomenal, daylong experience that included career coaching and a large community mural featuring a tree of life. We held the space for these young women to be together and talk about their visions for their lives.

From that point, I knew that I could never abandon my inner artist again. As I refined my business built around my Creative Mission, I leaned into my community-building skills. I built a space that welcomes those who've felt like outsiders, inviting them to remember their magic. It's a place where people break through their limitations to find honest, authentic self-expression. It's open-hearted, welcoming, and liberating in every way. This is the community of my dreams, and it's the space that I always needed that now I can provide for others.

My chosen communities are a magical mirror, reflecting myself back to me whenever I forget. Honestly, I still work through the same inner-child wounds and creative blocks. But when I find people who inspire me and show up for me, it makes me want to show up for them too. Together, we propel each other forward and find the fun in our process of our evolution and healing.

As a Radiant Wildheart, I embrace my differentness. I need to be around people who understand my Sacred Rebel spirit. For this reason, I'm selective about who I let in my inner circle.

I've connected with a vibrant community of people who are living their Creative Mission. These people are deep thinkers who respect my boundaries and remind me of the beauty I bring into the world. They are the people I feel comfortable enough with to express my emotions. They are the ones that see me and make me feel understood in all of my complexity. I've had to constantly work on my mindset to remind myself that those people are out there in abundance; I just have to find them. And no matter where you are, you can always find a handful of people who *get it* and who get you. When we find each other, we collaborate, share resources, promote each other. We aren't competing with each other because when one of us wins, we all win. And we go farther together.

When I didn't have a chosen community, I was caught up in a cycle of self-sabotage and isolation, trying to do this all on my own. But inside of me, there was always the longing to find belonging. To heal in community.

Expansion Exercise
SPIRALS OF SUPPORT

Just as your healing isn't linear, neither is your support system. There are many different types of support that you can draw upon to set yourself up for maximum success and bliss as you live your Creative Mission. I call this your **Spiral of Support**. These are the people you intentionally cultivate relationships with that will support you as you live your Creative Mission. It's not always easy to ask for support or even to recognize that we need it. But there are so many people in your life that can support you as you move throughout your journey.

It's time for you to get intentional about finding supportive relation-ships that help you live your Creative Mission. I want you to establish one or more of the following types of relationships in your life. Reach out to your trusted friends and invite them into this new way of relating with you. Make it sound fun and exciting. Enroll them in the possibility of being partners in transformation as you both live your Creative Mission.

This will probably feel a little vulnerable and scary at first, but it often results in magical connections that offer solid support. And if the person on the other end isn't interested or doesn't have the time, it's okay. Know that it doesn't mean anything about you or your worth. Find someone who is available and get committed to one another's growth.

The following are a few different types of supportive relationships you can create with your friends that will help you live your Creative Mission. Many people invest lots of money to find people in their lives to fulfill these roles. But if you find yourself in community with amazing beings, it doesn't have to cost you a thing and can be mutually supportive and symbiotically beneficial. It's a win-win-win, which we love here in the Radiant Wildheart community.

Fabulous Friendships

We all need to have friendships with those who grasp the truth of who we are. Your friends will be your adventure buddies and confidants. Friendship can be the most intimate and authentic relationship we have! They can also be some of the most resilient. Find friends who celebrate you and who want to see you win. People who you can relax and have fun with. Pour into your friendships and tend to them, and watch how that nourishes you too. Create a safe, supportive space for each other because you always need to have friends in this lifetime.

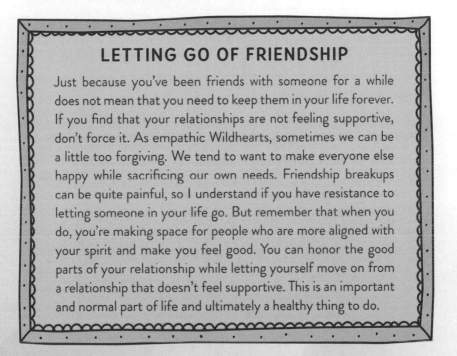

LETTING GO OF FRIENDSHIP

Just because you've been friends with someone for a while does not mean that you need to keep them in your life forever. If you find that your relationships are not feeling supportive, don't force it. As empathic Wildhearts, sometimes we can be a little too forgiving. We tend to want to make everyone else happy while sacrificing our own needs. Friendship breakups can be quite painful, so I understand if you have resistance to letting someone in your life go. But remember that when you do, you're making space for people who are more aligned with your spirit and make you feel good. You can honor the good parts of your relationship while letting yourself move on from a relationship that doesn't feel supportive. This is an important and normal part of life and ultimately a healthy thing to do.

Trusted Therapist

If you can, I recommend that everyone find time to chat with a licensed professional about your healing journey. When you are holding space for others, it's important to have someone hold you as well. It took a while to find the right therapist for me. Eventually, I found someone who shares a lot of the same identities as me, and that's helped me to unpack how what I'm moving through now relates to the bigger picture of my life. Your therapist is your safe space to process difficult emotions and helps you facilitate a healthy relationship with yourself.

You might be used to venting to your friends whenever something comes up that you need to process. But eventually, this will take a toll on your fabulous friendships and put yourself and your friends in a compromising situation. If you're moving through something difficult like unpacking or resolving trauma, your friends may not be qualified to give you advice on those topics. When you treat your friends like your therapist, you create an imbalance. It's best to seek out a professional, if possible. In your friendships, find the balance of being honest and authentic. You don't have to bypass the negative or anxiety-inducing things. But if you need deeper space holding or are seeking trauma resolution, I recommend finding a licensed professional to support you.

How to find mental health resources in your community:

- ✦ Check with your health insurance company to see if they cover mental health.
- ✦ Check with your local community centers for support groups and low-cost and sliding scale options for therapy.
- ✦ Find local resources for BIPOC, LGBTQ+, single parents, or any other group with which you identify.
- ✦ Check out your local LGBTQ+ center, which often provides mental health services and/or support groups
- ✦ Look for virtual therapists online.
- ✦ Try to find a mental health professional who makes you feel seen, understood, and safe.

Accountabilibuddies

An *accountabilibuddy* is my fun contraction for two words: accountability buddy. An accountabilibuddy can change your life. These are the people that help hold you accountable to do the work that you say is important to you. I've found that most of us need this extra layer of accountability to building the new habits that we know will bring us closer to accomplishing our goals. So much of the magic of transformation comes from consistently showing up for your practices overtime. And it helps a lot to have someone reaching out and checking in, helping you stay on track as you live your Creative Mission.

Being an accountabilibuddy is a commitment. It means you are willing to stand for your buddy and not allow them to flounder in their limitations and vice versa. It means that you hold a compassionate space but also remind them of the things they committed to and why. Find someone who you trust that you want to be your accountabilibuddy, and check in with each other about your progress. Find out what it is they want to accomplish next, and by when. Then hold them accountable to it.

MAKING THE MOST OUT OF YOUR ACCOUNTABILIBUDDY MEETINGS:

Here are some guidelines for how you can make your time together most effective.

+ Set up consistent meetings, e.g., weekly, biweekly, or monthly.

+ Map out a general meeting structure (perhaps you share a win, then spend 10 minutes talking about what you want to work on, then commit to your next step to accomplish before your next meeting).

+ Divide the time equally. If you are meeting for one hour, make sure you divide that hour evenly between each of you. Keep track of the clock, so one person

225

doesn't end up taking most of the time. It's important for your relationship that things feel equitable.

✦ Remember: This person is *not* your coach or your therapist! You are here to uplift each other. You need people who you can talk to about your Creative Mission! Do *not* spend the entire time complaining or venting. If you do, you're not being an effective accountabili-buddy, business bestie, or collaborator.

✦ Communicate about your needs. If you are meeting too often or not enough, say it! And say what you are thinking. If you notice your buddy is veering off into complaining-land, let them know. This time is for you as much as it is for them.

Business Besties

If you are an entrepreneur or aspire to be one, it's important that you maintain relationships with people who understand that aspect of your life. Entrepreneurship comes with some pretty unique gifts and challenges. When you are an entrepreneur, often you have so much to share about your business. All of the things that excite you and the things that you are struggling with.

Have a business bestie or two who are also entrepreneurs. It helps if they are in the same field or industry as you. These are people whose Creative Mission aligns with yours that you can meet with to discuss how you navigate entrepreneurship with the rest of your Radiant Wildheart life. Find people who inspire you and who are also committed to their liberation in this lifetime, and support each other as you reach for new levels of impact, embodiment, and success in your business.

Magical Mentors

Though we all come into the world knowing our gifts and how to express them, society conditions us to "forget." That's why we flounder when it's time to take our gifts to the next level. A mentor can show you the way to remembering your gifts. If there are new areas where you want to grow, one of the fastest ways to do that is with a guide who's walked the path before. A magical mentor will guide you through avoiding common mistakes as you make the leap into your next level of Greatness. They will inspire you with their own journey and continuously remind you that what you desire is possible and achievable. And they'll be living proof of that. Eventually, you will probably mentor people in your life as well!

GETTING MENTORSHIP

There are so many ways for you to find mentors and teachers to help you reach your next goal. First, get clear on exactly what goal you want to reach. What does your next level look like? Here are some options to help you learn more about what it will take to get there.

+ Find people who have accomplished that goal and ask if they'd be willing to share their knowledge with you.

+ Take classes virtually and locally to learn pretty much anything you want!

+ Seek out coaching or group mentorship programs to invest in that inspire you toward your desired outcome.

+ If all else fails, you can learn a lot from YouTube.

+ Learn for free or invest in getting the perfect kind of mentorship for you. The fastest way to get to your next destination is to find someone who has walked the path and can show you the way.

Creative Collaborators

You might find lots of creative synergy with the people in your Spiral of Support (more on that later). Be on the lookout for people who seem like they might have the potential to be a creative collaborator with you. These are people that you might want to lead a project with. People whose creativity inspires something in yours. Perhaps their Creative Mission is complementary to yours or perhaps they share about a topic that would enhance yours and bring new life to the conversation that you are interested in having in the world.

It's important that your creative collaborators are reliable and willing to create an equitable and fair collaborative relationship with you. I encourage you to start small with your creative collaborations—perhaps just a one-off collaborative livestream together or a single workshop, to see how your creative collaboration feels for you. From there, you can continue to dream up inspiring projects together and with others in your community. Ask yourself, *What kind of collaboration would feel easy, simple, and fun?* If a collaboration wants to happen and feels like an aligned step for you, go for it. See what kind of magic you can create with another inspired artist of life and how that might enhance your understanding of your Creative Mission.

Teaching

CULTIVATING #BUTTERFLYSKILLS

Revolutionizing your life starts with tending to your relationships. When you open your heart to create authentic connection, you will realize what amazing healing power there is in building with a team of people who are aligned to your vision. You and your chosen community will grow alongside each other. Your liberation will inform one another, and you will inspire each other to accomplish great things as individuals, together.

Many people move through life without people who understand their true value and the beauty they bring into the world. But it's up to you to intentionally nurture a garden of supportive relationships, and do the inner work that allows you to be truly seen. In order to do that, you must be willing to share with vulnerability. If you don't let us see the real you, how can we love you for it? As you share those genuine parts of yourself, even the ones that might feel a little tender, you'll attract people who are the right fit into your life. The more you are willing to live in your truth, the more you will find the aligned community of Wildhearts who unconditionally support you, because they know your heart, feel your commitment, and understand the journey you've been on.

Magical Mirrors

I see everyone inside my network as a magical mirror. When you can't remember your gifts, your chosen community will hold up that magical mirror to remind you exactly who you are. You shouldn't have to live your Creative Mission alone.

Everyone who shows up to the Wildheart community is a reflection. We are all equals. Just because I am the leader of the group doesn't mean that I am any more special or evolved than anyone else. Everyone in the Wildheart community brings an equally important thread that's essential to the tapestry we are weaving. Each person has incredible talents and creativity waiting to be unearthed and expressed. And, sometimes, this can be confronting.

My students will sometimes look around at the beauty and magic of those in the group and wonder if they belong. But if you are here and reading this, it's because you have the same amount of sparkle and that's why you've been attracted to this space. When you see another Wildheart being wildly expressed and living their truth, you might be tempted to compare yourself to them. But if you can see their inner light, it's because that same light is inside of you too. You are a magical mirror of them, and vice versa.

The Wildhearts are a team. One person's success is all of our success. One person's challenges belong to all of us. I encourage all Wildhearts to celebrate one another and take up lots of space with #BrilliantBrags. I want us to have the opportunity to shine brightly without dimming that inner light. Because when we shine, it doesn't take away from anyone else's magic. In fact, it enhances it. Seeing you in your radiant glory and sparkling energy amplifies our own magic by inspiring us and reminding us of what's possible, especially if we might have momentarily forgotten.

In most spaces, everyone, especially femme-identifying folks, are shamed for celebrating their accomplishments. We are told that if we do, we're conceited. But when someone else is winning, it shows us that we can too. So I want you to celebrate your success loudly and cheer each other on. You deserve a space to be seen and celebrated in all of your accomplishments. Your chosen community can provide that space for you, and you can provide it for them too. And that is such a gift.

Find ways to show your support. Like and share their posts (#signalboost!) and speak highly of your fellow Wildhearts, even when they're not in the room. Make it an intentional practice to be a generous community member and watch how it enriches your life and circles back around to create even more abundance for you too.

INNER OVERPROTECTOR
The Lone Wolf

Meet the Lone Wolf. Lone Wolves are used to doing things on their own. They often feel misunderstood and tend to reject the world before the world can reject them. The Lone Wolf is highly individual and resists asking for help along the journey. Similarly, they're wary of getting close with other people. They might make friends, but they hold back from being authentically vulnerable. And we know that vulnerability is what creates real connections.

Lone Wolves feel like they need to do everything on their own because they don't trust that others will understand how to do things the right way. Because of their distrusting nature, this Inner Overprotector tends to make you miss out on the abundant opportunities that come from being a part of a team. The Lone Wolf might burn out or even burn bridges because they don't think you need others. But this is just a protective mechanism because they are afraid of being rejected. Let your Lone Wolf know that you are going to keep them safe while you find your chosen community.

You might be experiencing the Lone Wolf if:

+ You assume that no one will really understand you, so you don't bother trusting people.

+ You feel like an outsider who is unique and nontraditional.

+ You get easily triggered by other people and are quick to write them off or cut them out of your life.

+ You're so attached to being different that you reject opportunities for real intimacy or community.

+ You tend to isolate yourself but then find yourself feeling lonely.

Tips for Dealing with the Lone Wolf:

+ Set up a time to connect with a friend with absolutely no agenda but to just hang out and have fun. Can you make these friend dates a weekly practice?

+ Reach out to someone that you haven't spoken to in a while just to check in and see how they are doing. Start showing up for your friendships in more intentional ways.

+ Set parameters around your working hours and technology usage so that you aren't on the phone or computer late into the night. If you have time away from technology, you may find that you have more space to build intimate connections with the people in your life.

❧❧❧ CREATIVE PRACTICE ❧❧❧
Art Project
MAKE YOUR OWN SPIRAL OF SUPPORT

Now that you've explored the different components of your Spiral of Support system, it's time to start creating. Find a blank sheet of paper and start to create your own Spiral of Support. You can put your sacred self in the center, and around you draw rings for all of the different types of support listed in the previous sections. Within each ring, note who in your life already fulfills those roles for you. If you don't have someone yet, write down the qualities you're looking for in the people you want to manifest into your life and into those roles.

The first step to getting what you want is naming it. What kind of community and support systems do you desire to make your creative dreams a reality? Make this Spirals of Support artwork as colorful and magical as you like. Decorate and adorn it. Once you're done, hang it up in your creative workspace as a reminder of all of the different options you have to be fully supported to live your Creative Mission.

Archetype Spotlight

BUILDING YOUR COMMUNITY

 MYSTIC—You want to find and connect with others who are as connected to the ethereal realm as you are so you can fully express that side of you. There might be people in your life that are less interested in the woo-woo topics that you're drawn to, and that's okay. But you do need to find people who you can vibe with spiritually for you to feel fully seen and understood. Find those multidimensional starseeds and lightworkers that remind you of your true nature and role in the universe.

 VISIONARY—You are at your best when you are connecting and uplifting others. Your airy nature makes you adept at being a social butterfly and a natural networker. You have a gift for being able to see the bigger vision and help others find their own Creative Mission and way to serve in this world. You create so many opportunities for yourself and others with your ability to network and socialize. Don't shy away from it. If you see someone who you know might be a positive influence in your life, don't be afraid to reach out with a compliment or anything that might help build those connections. You never know where they may lead.

 SACRED REBEL—You tend to be a lone wolf and feel a bit different from others. You might feel like people rarely understand you, and this can mean that you miss out on amazing connections that could support your vision even more. As a fiery being, you are a powerful force of nature. We are drawn by your passion, but sometimes you can be a little self-focused. You are so used to marching to the beat of your own drum that you might not realize how many other Radiant Wildhearts there are for you to play and collaborate with. Remember that you don't have to do this alone. Set the intention to let your trusted friends in just a little bit more. Be a little more vulnerable and connected and watch how it improves your quality of life.

 HEALER—You are naturally a Healer and might find yourself holding an emotional space for others that's as deep as the ocean. This is such a beautiful gift that you provide, but don't forget that you need someone to hold you in your process as well. Have you reached out to your Spiral of Support lately? Have you connected with your business besties or a trusted therapist? Also, don't forget the importance of holding your own energetic boundaries when people are emotionally processing with you. Don't be afraid to lovingly let people know what you are and aren't available for, so that you can preserve your own energy and protect your peace of mind.

 GUARDIAN—You have a powerful energy that people are attracted to. So many people are drawn to the safe space that you hold. And you are absolutely loyal to the people in your life that you adore. Are you clear about who those people are that make you feel your most empowered? How about the ones that encourage you to share your gifts and get out of your comfort zone? What about the people who remind you to be gentle on yourself? There are lots of amazing people in your life, and you get to choose the connections that encourage you to shine your earthly magic. Since you tend to be the reliable one for those in your life, I want to invite you to cultivate some of these productive connections that pour into you also.

CHAPTER TWELVE

Embodiment

Walk Your Talk and Live Your Message Out Loud

Every time I stood in front of my first visual arts classroom, my bright-eyed elementary school students saw me in my magic: bold, fully expressed, colorful, and unafraid to be myself. They looked up to me in every way.

What they didn't know was that most of the time, I was hearing the voices of my Inner Overprotectors. And when I stepped up to the whiteboard to draw an example, I panicked on the inside, afraid that I would mess up in front of everyone. But no matter what happened or how many mistakes I made, my students loved me and everything I stood for, even when I couldn't see it in myself. As I move through life, their perceptions of me are always in my heart and spirit, lifting me up and reminding me of why I choose to face my fear of being seen in my creativity.

That doesn't mean everything is sunshine and butterflies for me now. I still get nervous or second-guess myself, but it doesn't stop me from doing what I am guided to do. I teach creativity because it's what I most need to learn. I dedicated my life to my muses and never looked back.

There are weeks when I slip back into old patterns of being too busy to create or tend to my inner child and her big emotions. But now, I notice more quickly when I'm slipping out of alignment with my truth. And it's a lot easier to bring myself back to my path because I have so many magical tools in my toolbox that I've cultivated over the years. The more I've learned to work with my Inner Overprotectors, the more I'm able to stand confidently in the Creative Mission that wants to be expressed through me.

Looking back, I realize that I knew so much more than I gave myself credit for. Because I took my seat as a teacher without feeling "ready," I ended up learning a lot on the fly. Sometimes you have to take the leap only to discover your wings on the way down. This made me nimble, channeling impactful lessons and making things up as I went in order to get the job done. I came up against challenges, mistakes, and plenty of surprises, but I didn't have time to dwell on the fear or my suffering. I had no choice but to figure it out, and fast.

As I grew my business, I kept that same energy, leading with my intuition when I didn't have the answer. I mastered the art of channeling truth and creativity from a place inside of me that was a lot more powerful than those cute little Inner Overprotectors. Surprisingly, many of the things that I discovered when I thought I was just making things up ended up being totally true and resonated with a lot of people.

It didn't take long for me to realize that to be fully expressed, I needed to finally stop living from my head and lead with my heart. And this is still a constant practice of noticing when I'm trying to think my way to an answer and choose a more magical path. When I ground into my body's wisdom, I can create miraculous results from a place of ease and overflow. Because I chose to teach and share, I also chose to be on a powerful self-initiation journey of casting spells with my words and speaking about what I wanted to be true—the world as I wished to see it.

From there, the universe has shown me exactly where I needed to come into greater alignment. And I began to see my reflection in others, the people who resonated with my Creative Mission and who were walking a similar path but a bit farther ahead. That was so healing. Because if others are inherently creative, worthy, and resourceful, so am I.

To embody my Creative Mission, I had to release the part of me that thinks success is linked to how much I produce, work, and accomplish. I made intentional space in my life to slow down so that my creativity can flow. I dance more. I sing more. I nap more. And I've even managed to write an entire book about the creative process. I've been painting more than ever. All of this creativity has informed my teaching practice and vice versa. And sometimes I still fall out of my creative practice. And that's okay because every day I have another opportunity to bring myself back to these magical tools.

I am constantly embodying deeper levels of my truth and releasing everyone else's opinions so that I can finally do what works for me. Because my life has shown me that I will be the best version of myself when I create a world around me that wants me to thrive. I'm finally working on my first music album and am embodying my inner artist on a whole new level. One that's sourced from a deeper place inside of me. Where I don't have to try or strive because my creativity just flows. It's in every word that I speak, every breath that I take, and everything that I touch. My entire life is blessed. I am art in motion and nothing will ever change that.

What I find the most interesting is that as I look back on my life, having only done creative things for work and eventually building a creative business around it, I realize that I've been channeling the exact same message for well over a decade. I see old posts on Facebook from when I was an art teacher where I talk about how I am leaving my job to pursue my dreams.

> **Shereen Sun** was ⚪ celebrating life.
> 29 April 2015 · 👥
>
> OK! The e-mail has been sent. I am not taking the Summer position I planned for in order to more seriously commit to being guided by my passions & create my dream. I have been talking about this for a long time and the time has come. Yay ☺ Wish me luck. More to come....

Facebook post where I let the world know that
I was not going to be pursuing another school teaching job

I didn't know exactly what it meant, but clearly I was hearing a call that hasn't gone away. I see older videos from the early years of my Radiant Wildheart career where I say with such conviction that your life and business is meant to be a radical act of creativity. And that the more fun you have, the bigger an impact and more money you will create. At the time, I was channeling these messages. I didn't have a lot of lived experience to back up those claims, but something inside of me told me it was true. I didn't even fully understand these messages until now. I'm still embodying the wisdom in what's been coming through my Creative Mission in deeper ways. But I can see that for all of these years, since the first moment I said yes to the inspired ideas that were coming through me, my Creative Mission has stayed pretty consistent.

So, Wildheart, the answers that you seek really are within you. And the way to get to where you want to go isn't necessarily by having a well thought-out plan of action. It's through embodiment. It's through the practice of listening deeply to what your life is trying to tell you, trusting and following it. Instead of overanalyzing and trying to figure out the "how," focus on embodying the very message that you wish to share. When you do, your inner wisdom will guide you to your next step.

I've built an incredible network of inspired Radiant Wildhearts who do work that matters. I love taking creative classes, finding mentors, and reading books by those living in their Creative Mission so that I can discover what keys they've unlocked on their journey. I love to learn from other artists. This is why I got my undergraduate degree in art history. By studying the journey of other artists walking their Divine Purpose Path, we can build on their legacy and find new ways toward our own embodied self-expression.

I'm not waiting for someone to save me, rescue me, or give me all the answers. I know that my teachers are humans like the rest of us, and it's never healthy to put someone on a pedestal above you. I don't seek to emulate anyone else and am committed to finding my own creative frequency and a vibe that only I can bring. I let others support me and show me new ways to become a more expressed version of myself. I trust my creativity and embodied wisdom to guide me to where I need to go.

When I live from this energy that I've been intentionally cultivating and curating, I spark my own internal creative revolution. Through my practice of embodiment, I've been able to open up to the more subtle cues that my creative spirit gives me. The presence that's available to me in each breath. In the pleasure I experience on a slow morning and the love I feel from the Radiant Wildhearts that I truly connect with. Every day is an opportunity to find the bliss, laughter, and connection that I've been seeking for my entire life. And it starts from within, and then my outer reality becomes a reflection of it. A by-product of living life on my terms is that I get to invite others to join the party. I don't have to work harder or longer hours. I can change the world just by being my magical self. It really is that simple.

Teaching

EMBODY WHAT YOU WISH TO TEACH

Almost every student I've ever worked with has moved through a deep, dark night of the soul, wondering if they are capable. Most of the time, the exact things that they struggle with are the very things they desire to teach. For example, the leadership trainer who finds herself people-pleasing and having boundary issues. Or the creativity mentor who is mimicking other coaches instead of diving into their own ideas. Or the spiritual mentor who has lost faith that anyone will ever want to hire them for their services. I see this over and over again. Often, I've seen my students grapple with the persistent thought that if they are struggling, how can they possibly teach and share? Cue #impostorsyndrome.

I always tell them, "We teach what we most need to learn." The thing is, every time you step out of your comfort zone, you're going to be faced with these same challenges. The universe is putting these challenges in front of you for you to break through them once and for all. Sure, you could turn back now because it's uncomfortable, but what good would that do? Every time you try to accomplish something great, these same issues are going to pop up again and again until you move through them.

If something has been calling to you to share, it might be because you are being asked to heal it in this lifetime. I teach creativity because it's the medicine that I need, but that doesn't mean it comes easily to me. The best way to get to the root of these challenges and blocks is to be totally devoted to your liberation. You deserve to break free from these thought patterns that aren't serving you. And the only way out is through. Most of the time, your Creative Mission is calling for you to transform your greatest challenges into your greatest assets.

The only way to get there is to practice what you preach. When you step into your Creative Mission, the universe will hold you accountable, making sure you walk your talk and live it every day. Many of my students get hung up for months, trying to find the perfect way to describe their work. They ask me questions about the right words to use to explain what they do in their "elevator pitch," which is meant to succinctly express one's Creative Mission.

Sounds simple, right? But often, this assignment stumps people for way too long. It's not easy to capture your embodied essence into one simple sentence. So I tell them to forget about it. Let it go. And instead focus on becoming the message they wish to share.

Focusing on embodiment is so much juicier. When you try to put perfect words to your Creative Mission, you're living in your head. You're trying to "get it right" and focusing externally on how everyone else will perceive what you do. But that analytical part of your mind has kept you second-guessing yourself this entire time. And it's probably time to intentionally shut it off for a moment and let your heart's wisdom lead the way. I find that when I do this embodiment work with my clients, the answers just flow from a deeper place. Questions that may have had people stumped for months suddenly get answered in moments. Embody the topic you wish to share. Be about it, and let it teach you. When you do, your energy will be more congruent with your message. And others will feel that alignment too.

Wildheart, only you have the power to heal your mindset. The universe wants to support you in living your Creative Mission. But first you have to hold yourself accountable to trusting in this fact and believing that what you want, wants you. You are being asked to take radical responsibility for your healing and mindset so that you can be a magnet for everything you want and repel everything you don't.

I've given you the tools to break through your perceived limitations into full self-expression. But no matter how much positive feedback you get, at the end of the day, if you don't feel it in your heart first, you won't believe the praise. You deserve to make an impact doing what you love. Analyzing your way out of your fears won't create a lasting change in your thinking and behavior. Trusting that what you seek is seeking you in every fiber of your being is the first step to manifesting your desires in this lifetime.

I would rather see you fully nourished and creatively inspired, feel you as a beacon of hope and possibility, and experience you in your presence rather than view your perfectly crafted website. Your worth is not linked to how much you produce. Here in the Radiant Wildheart community, we believe in quality over quantity. Your miraculous results and fabulous impact will be a direct result of your authentic energy and the presence that you bring to every situation.

If there's any hint of self-doubt lingering, that's your cue to go even deeper into your practices. When you notice that you're feeling a desperate need for validation, or you're having a hard time finding the faith that everything is working out in your favor, take it as a message from the universe. If you're not feeling abundant or overflowing, it's likely time to slowly back away from the laptop and choose self-care instead. We all experience these moments of misalignment, but the real magic is in how you respond to them to transmute that energy into something that heals you.

Use the wonderful tools in your magical toolbox to move that energy and come out on the other side. Journal, make art about your feelings, or talk to your accountabilibuddy or trusted therapist. When you do, you're going to notice the shift. It might be small or big, but over time with consistency, those intentional moments are going to help you embody your message with such beauty and power that we will all be mesmerized.

Expansion Exercise
TAKE UP SPACE: BRILLIANT BRAGS
& YOUR BEAUTIFUL SELF

Celebrate some of your wins and successes in your Abundance Journal. Can you name 100 things you are proud of yourself for? Most of the time, we don't give ourselves enough credit for all the amazing things we've created and instead focus on where we could improve. But there's so much about you that's worth bragging about and celebrating. Let this assignment be an empowering one where you revel in your accomplishments, acknowledge the things you've created, and see the challenges you've transmuted along the way. You have so much to be proud of yourself for! I hope that after completing this exercise, you can *see* yourself a bit more clearly.

Bonus: Once you've journaled and taken some time to celebrate yourself, find a trusted friend or accountabilibuddy to share some of these wins with. Note in your Abundance Journal what it felt like to be witnessed loving yourself and your journey. Did you notice anything interesting? If so, what?

INNER OVERPROTECTOR

The Copycat

It's time to meet the Copycat! The Copycat mimics other people. They might have borrowed the work of your favorite teachers, healers, or coaches. They try on other people's Creative Missions and identities because they think it will make you more successful. They're not bitter or trying to be malicious. The Copycat subconsciously devalues your true self and message because they want to protect you from rejection. Your creativity is so vulnerable and precious, and if someone rejects it that would hurt the Copycat quite a bit. But as you and I both know, this isn't the right energy to get you to where you want to be.

Your Creative Mission is unique to you. Most artists will agree that imitating others is a normal part of the creative process. But now it's time for you to move past that. While you can certainly try to be like other people and be inspired by their journey, it's only going to get you so far. If you want to live in your most expansive creative expression, it has to come from deep within you. And it is going to be a Creative Mission that only you can accomplish.

Instead of looking outward at everyone else, spend time with your own creative practice. This is where you will get to know yourself. Build something that has your unique energetic imprint on it. Tell your story. Trust me, even though others might have a similar story, no one can tell it like you can. And there are lots of people out there who are waiting for someone just like you to take up space, because they will resonate a lot with your authentic journey. If the voice of the Copycat has its claws in you, don't shame yourself for it. Instead, set the intention to find your own style and stay true to it.

You might be experiencing the Copycat if:

✦   You're constantly looking at what others are doing for cues on what you should create next.

✦   You feel like you need to be just like your mentors or inspirations to be successful.

✦   You fear that your ideas won't be well received by the people you long to serve.

✦   You second-guess yourself and are afraid to follow your own heart.

✦   You repeat information that you've heard elsewhere without putting an original spin on it.

Tips for Dealing with the Copycat:

Here's a self-assessment practice for you: Get honest with yourself! Who do you look up to? Who are the people you follow who are living the kind of life you want to live? Examine where you are trying to be like them. Call yourself out on this with love. Are you using the language that they use, even though it doesn't feel authentic to you? Are you trying to teach what they teach the way they teach it?

When you imitate someone, you often know you are doing it, and it doesn't feel fully authentic. Take a moment here to self-reflect if you've been consciously or subconsciously imitating someone you admire. Then reimagine your movement so that it feels more like you and less like other people. How can you bring more of your authentic energy into it?

"I am my own muse. I am the subject I know best. The subject I want to know better."

— OROMA ELEWA

CREATIVE PRACTICE
Star Power Self-Portrait

Star power is the magical charisma and confidence that some people radiate. Many celebrities and rock stars have a certain essence. They emanate badass, Radiant Wildheart energy. They're unapologetic and clear about who they are. Each person's star power is different. Your star power is going to be unique to you. You don't have to be loud or bold to have star power. Some rock stars have a more introverted appeal. But they still show up as powerful, with a depth to their energetic presence that makes us all lean in and want to know what's going on in their minds.

In this creative practice, you're going to use the medium of self-portraiture. Self-portraits are powerful! Your self-portrait doesn't have to look realistic but instead can be a representation of how you see your archetypal self—or how you'd want to be seen in all of your creative magic. For this creative practice, you are going to use photography to make a self-portrait, demonstrating yourself in your star power, your most magical self and as you want to be seen in the world.

This exercise is meant to be fun. Take a moment to consider what you, in your absolute Star Power Magic, would look like. If you were your most expressed self, what would you look like? What would you wear? What setting would you be in? While this might feel like you're channeling your alter ego, you're actually channeling another aspect of yourself. Now is your time to express and give space to the parts of yourself that you may have kept hidden. Now is the time to put an image to what it would look like if you were to fully let your star power shine.

1. Take some time to do your embodiment practices. Turn up music that you love and have a solo dance party. Get into those hips. Stretch it out and practice taking up more space. Breathe with one hand on your heart and one hand on your belly as you sink even deeper into your embodied self. Touch your skin as you move. Let your senses deepen as you find more presence.

2. Find an outfit that makes you feel fully expressed, confident, and radiating your Radiant Wildheart energy. Choose your look based on who you know you truly are, not how you normally dress or show up in your day-to-day life. This is a special occasion. Push past the edge of your comfort zone and set the intention to go wild, whatever that means to you. Is the vibe fierce? Colorful? Elegant? Powerful? Show us what it looks like. Perhaps you choose some props that are meaningful for you or put on some makeup in a way that feels expressive of the energy you want to convey.

3. Now it's time to shoot. You are both the artist and the subject, and no one has to see these photos but you. Set up your camera and do your Star Power Self-Portrait Photoshoot. Have as much fun as possible, and be sure to continue to stretch out of your comfort zone. The longer you shoot, the more comfortable you will feel. Keep looking back at the photos and see how they feel. Remember, the point is to have fun and create something authentic, so if you get caught up in your head, revisit one of your embodiment practices and come back to this afterward.

Let this be a wildly creative experiment. Know that you don't have to share these photos with anyone. But, if you want to, you can share your self-portraits online. Hashtag them #radiantwildheart so that I can see them! I can't wait to witness you in all of your star power and celebrate you taking up lots of space with your magic. We are so blessed to get to experience your self-expression in this lifetime!

Representation

TAKE UP SPACE BY TELLING YOUR STORY

We live in a world that bombards us with images and stories that only depict a very specific type of person. Usually, we see representations of people who are white, thin, nondisabled, and straight. But you and I both know most of us don't fit into this stereotypical demographic. So why is this the vast majority of what we see?

In the past, media was severely gatekept. Those who wanted to tell stories that represented people with diverse identities were not given access. The marginalized characters we did see were often fetishized, one-dimensional, stereotypical, and just downright offensive. For some, these depictions were their only experience of certain groups of people.

I remember how much I longed to see people like me in movies, TV, and media. But I rarely did. When I did stumble upon another queer South Asian American artist to look up to, I relished in it. It meant the world to me. I settled for any kind of representation and found myself binging on queer movies and music so I could feel less alone.

So many of us grew up feeling like we didn't belong. If you're queer or from a marginalized community, you know what it feels like to have to pretend to be something that you're not in order to fit in. We got used to going into spaces that didn't want to consider us as important. So we did what we could to assimilate, even if that meant abandoning essential parts of our identity. Combine that with the fact that we didn't see anyone like us in the media, and this assimilation felt like life or death.

We've lived in fear that if people found out the truth of who we are, we would be cast out of our communities. Lack of representation leads to disparities in mental wellness and personal achievement. It creates anxiety, depression, and a pattern of settling for much less than we deserve.

It's clear that things are finally changing because we're demanding it. Many influential BIPOC and LGBTQ+ creators are now telling their stories. We're creating the media we needed to see growing up. Now I'm stoked to see that diverse stories are becoming a trend. Organizations and businesses finally want to be on the right side of history. That means this is the right time and place for you to own your voice and create the media you've always needed. All it takes is a phone camera and a wifi connection to spark your own creative revolution.

Now that every one of us has the power to create our own media, you can take up space in the world. You can influence the world by telling your story. And when you do, you'll be showing the youth of today that it's okay to be different and that they're not alone. You're doing your part to make the world a more inclusive, safer place for people like you and me. And that in itself is so rewarding. So own your voice, Wildheart!

It's not an accident that every chapter of this book begins with me telling a few of my stories. Stories are how we connect with one another. As humans, we understand the world through storytelling. One of the most common mistakes that I see my clients make is only sharing big, abstract ideas about the collective but not about their own personal journey.

When I see someone doing this, I know it's because they're afraid. (I know this because I've been there!) It's a lot easier to hide behind big universal theories than to talk about your own story, especially the more vulnerable parts. While yes, it's true that our planet is experiencing a shift in consciousness, the only way to be a part of that shift is to be willing to let people into the aspects of your life that you probably aren't used to sharing.

To be clear, I don't mean you need to have one perfectly crafted narrative of your life that you can share from a stage. I want you to get connected to the wild and beautiful experiences you've lived through. Your entire life is filled with millions of stories. You've probably shared many of them with your best friends and those closest to you. If you're not sure where to begin, it's probably because you haven't spent enough time with your stories, but it's not too late to start exploring them.

At this point, I've written my stories, spoken them out loud, and felt deeply witnessed by strangers as well as people who've known me forever. This used to scare me, and in a lot of ways, it still does. But I know I must create the media that I want to see in the world. The more I have been willing to share, the more I have integrated and embodied all of the experiences that make me who I am. I got more comfortable in my identity, and it's been a bonus that doing so has helped lots of other people too.

Trust me when I say that you have lots of valuable stories that the world needs to hear. Learning how to tell those stories is essential for you to become fully embodied in your Creative Mission. As you are seen in your stories, you'll start to integrate them even more.

An added benefit to telling your story is that you'll find a more aligned chosen community to build with. I've created such a beautiful community of like-minded creators. We collaborate together and build friendships too. These are the types of people I've always wanted to be friends with. They're interested in healing, creativity, queerness, sexuality, and all the things that truly light me up. Their content inspires me and vice versa. There's a mutual respect between us that is so uplifting.

I found these creators because I've been willing to talk openly about myself. These Wildhearts hold a magical space for me in my process. The more I created and shared my journey, thoughts, and offerings that were truly aligned with the stories I've lived through, the more the right people showed up to cheer me on. And I've talked to many other Wildhearts who've experienced the same phenomenon. When you are willing to share and tell your story, the right people will somehow magically find you.

Your story may inspire others to come out of a particular closet. It can remind others that it's okay to be different. While it might feel stretchy AF at first, the more you do it, the easier it will become. And when you practice fully living in your truth by being seen and telling your story, you will quickly become the most resilient version of yourself. Wildheart, you can change the world just by being you.

Archetype Spotlight
EMBODYING YOUR MESSAGE

 MYSTIC—Your connection to spirit is powerful and revolutionary, but only if you are able to remain grounded here on Earth. Remember that you are on this planet in a body for a reason, and that reason has everything to do with your Creative Mission. Try practicing grounding exercises: things like energetically sending your roots into the earth or putting your bare feet on the ground outside. Simple grounding practices don't have to take more than a couple of minutes but can make a huge difference on your day, clarity, and focus.

 VISIONARY—You have the airy tendency to say yes to lots of creative projects and ideas that light you up. This is beautiful but requires practice and patience so that you don't become overwhelmed or stuck in your head. No matter how much of a creative genius you are, if you are spread thin with too much on your plate, you're going to be severely limiting your impact and taking away from your ability to be fully embodied in your message. Take extra care to preserve your space and carve out free time for yourself to do nothing but be present, whatever that means in a given moment. It might be hard at first to leave all of this empty space in your schedule, but eventually you will see what an improvement it makes on your embodiment and peace of mind.

 SACRED REBEL—As someone who is so driven by intense emotions like passion and transformation, it's essential that you move all of the energy inside of your body so it has somewhere to go! Try to find ways to express yourself through movement, dance, or any other embodiment practice that speaks to you.

Let yourself twirl in the flames of transformation and give yourself an opportunity to be free and shake off anything that's no longer serving you.

HEALER—The most important thing you can learn is how to clear other people's energy off of you. You can be energetically spongy and tend to hold on to people's emotions for them. You might even hold on to energy from people walking by you or in spaces that you enter. As such, it's so important that you clear your energy often. There are lots of ways to cleanse, clear, and protect your spirit. A few examples are to take a nice salt bath, burn some copal, or ring a bell and tune in to the sound-healing frequencies. Practicing these clearing and cleansing rituals will allow you to come back to your own energy, so you're not holding on to other people's baggage and can tap into what's truly yours to share.

GUARDIAN—You are naturally very grounded, which is wonderful. But you would benefit from connecting to the divine and your spirit team. Open your crown chakra and allow yourself to connect to the cosmic energy that's always available to you. Take time to look up at the sky or the stars, do a ritual on the full moon, and let yourself enjoy some magical cosmic energy. Let yourself lighten up and call on your guides and higher self to allow your grounded vibes to intermingle with all of the celestial energy soaring up above. This balance will support you to share your Creative Mission with more freedom and joy.

Conclusion

Empowered Expression in Life and Leadership

Congratulations, you magical Radiant Wildheart. I want to celebrate you deeply for all the work and play that you've put in so far. It's a huge accomplishment to reach the conclusion of this book, and we in the Radiant Wildheart community are beyond proud of you. You've taken a magical journey toward wild self-expression and full embodiment of your Radiant Wildheart. Now it's your turn to celebrate yourself. Look back on your journey and consider the many intentional steps you took to get here. Think back to all of the healing, the breakthroughs, the challenges, and the blessings that led you up to this point.

This is a journey that most people have not had the blessing to embark on. But here you are, a more liberated version of yourself. You've intentionally called upon your spirit team and asked for their guidance as you step more deeply onto your Divine Purpose Path. You've taken the time to understand your inner artist, and you're now equipped with the tools to take your Creative Mission out into the world and play. You've listened to your intuition more deeply and taken action accordingly—and now look at all of the amazing transformations that have taken place in such a short amount of time. Take a moment to really breathe in this new reality. You did that. You've crossed a sacred threshold into a whole new chapter of your life where nothing is more important than you living your truth.

You are now feeling intimately connected to yourself as an artist. You're able to separate yourself from the voices of your Inner Overprotectors.

You now have so many tools in your magical toolbox to help you love yourself through any challenge that comes your way. Your devotion and commitment to your growth shows. It emanates from you and fills up every room that you walk into with magic and messages of hope. You probably don't even realize how much your embodiment inspires those around you, but it does. You've gone inward to reflect and come out with a beautiful understanding of what your Creative Mission is and how you wish to serve. And with every step you take, you are expressing that Creative Mission in the world, and it makes a difference. You might not realize it now, but your embodiment and way of being is going to impact so many people that you connect with. And because of you, they will go out and impact people in their lives and community. And together, we create such a colorful ripple effect on the planet that is so needed.

For me, this is what makes life truly meaningful. To be a part of something bigger. An integral piece of this collaborative web we are weaving. It's truly so beautiful to witness your growth and my heart sings for you and for the world, because now we get to experience your gifts in all of their glory. This world wouldn't be the same without your contributions.

It's time to celebrate. Celebrating yourself is an essential part of the creative cycle. The juiciness of a good old-fashioned party will reinspire and replenish your energy after all of the hard work you've done to show up! If you don't take the time to celebrate yourself and your wins, you won't have anything to reset and prepare you for the next cycle of your creative journey and all of the healing that comes along with it. But when you do take the time to luxuriate in your accomplishments and treat yourself for all of your growth—big or small, you'll be filled with abundant energy to start this process all over again from a new place.

Wildheart, the work is never over, and this is only the beginning. I know that you have transformed in such profound ways. But living as your Radiant Wildheart self is lifetime work. There's no mythical end destination where you will finally feel enlightened. Healing is a spiral, and we circle back to certain lessons over and over again. Even the creatives you admire need to come back to the themes discussed within this book. We all have moments where we get stuck and need a reminder of what we are capable of. So don't be surprised if there are moments where you once again feel unsure of your gifts. Don't be alarmed if you find that you have once again fallen out of your creative practice for months, or even years. It happens. Even to me. All the time.

Just because you've read this guide doesn't mean that all of your habits and patterns have shifted forever. If only it were so simple. The practice of your creativity requires a continual recommitment. And as you reach new levels of liberation, you're going to come across new challenges that might have you working through new levels of resistance. And that's okay. That's a part of the process too. It's very common and normal. And every step of your journey is sacred.

As a Radiant Wildheart, you are now committed to the path of continual growth, learning, and creative evolution. You get to stay devoted to your inner artist and continue to cultivate the creative practices that bring so much healing and self-reflection to your life. And you get to find new and more aligned ways to share those gifts with the world in whatever way feels right for you at the time. Your Creative Mission will evolve alongside you, so if you feel the winds of change coming, embrace them and stay curious about what your next aligned steps might be. When things shift, you're not starting over from scratch. You're just refining things even more. Each of these changes are bringing you closer to fully living your truth.

The Radiant Wildheart Community is here for you. You aren't alone and you don't have to do this in isolation. We cordially invite you to join our movement of creating a more colorful and inclusive world. When you approach your Creative Mission the Radiant Wildheart way, your nervousness will transform into excitement. You'll have a lot of fun getting liberated. And even if you're a little scared, you'll have so many reminders in the form of your friends and muses to remind you why you are choosing to walk this path. And of course, you've got your lovable spirit team in the invisible realms to energetically support you the entire time, as long as you make sure to ask for their guidance whenever you need it.

Don't worry if you didn't complete every single practice or read every page of this book. You don't need to. We love being perfectly imperfect around here. This process is not linear, and you don't need to complete all of the steps in order. If you skipped some, perhaps you'll find time to reflect on where your resistance was to that practice and then schedule some time to try it out in the future. This book is always here for you to come back to, and I do recommend reading and rereading it. Keep it somewhere where you can see it, so that even when you're not reading it, you can be positively impacted just by its energy.

What does it mean to be liberated in this lifetime? Only you can answer that question. But now that you've gotten to know yourself on such a deep level, you can use this information to optimize your entire life and attune to the unique way that you receive insights. The reason why you are doing this work is so that you can feel truly fulfilled and thrive in this lifetime. And that fulfillment is going to be yours and yours alone. It doesn't matter what anyone has to say about your life, how you express yourself, or your Creative Mission. At the end of the day, you will be the one that knows when you are living in integrity and alignment with your inner artist. You are the one that needs to feel fulfilled and expressed in order to make the impact that you came here to make.

You have earned your graduation. I offer deep bows of honor for where you have been, who you have become, and who you are becoming. I'm so grateful for you saying yes to your Creative Mission and so honored to walk this path with you. And I am celebrating this new version of you and your commitment to embody the healing that you've been longing for.

I hope you're all the way hyped about what is yet to come. When you align your life with your creativity, miracles are possible. Everything you're calling in is on its way to you. So be patient and look out for all the synchronicities and messages. You are divinely guided. You are art in motion. You are infinitely blessed!

Welcome to the first day of the rest of your life.

P.S. I've made you a certificate of completion that you can print and hang up on your wall as a reminder of your journey. To check it out, visit **www.radiantwildheart.com/gifts.**

Glorious Glossary

Language is so magical. Throughout this book I'll echo "words cast spells," and it's true. The way we speak about our lives and Creative Missions makes a huge difference in the ways we carry ourselves. There are many words in this book that have been intentionally imbued with my own definitions. Some of these words might be unfamiliar to you, so I've created this handy glossary for you to get a deeper look into how I define them. I encourage you to be more intentional about the language you use on a regular basis to describe your creative self. You have the power to come up with your own definitions and word combinations, so that language always brings you closer to your desired vibration.

Abundance Journal: Any kind of magical notebook that makes you feel absolutely abundant. Mine has gold leaves and feels fancy. Carry it with you to jot down all your inspired ideas. Fill your Abundance Journal with the inner workings of your brilliant mind and shining heart, so you can always reflect on your growth.

Anti-racism: The practice of creating policies, practices, ideologies, and worldviews that eliminate racism at the individual and structural levels.

Creative Dream: A vision for your life that represents your hopes and deep desires. It brings you lots of joy and excitement when you think about it, and it's probably something that you would do for free. Every single person is walking around on this planet with a creative dream.

Many people feel the pull of their creative dreams moving them toward something, and often those feelings don't ever go away.

Creative Mission: Where your creativity intersects with your drive to make a difference in this world. Every single person on this planet arrives with a sacred Creative Mission—the reason why you are here that was whispered into your ear before you were born.

Creativity: Open-ended, a way of life, and a state of mind; a lens through which you can look at absolutely anything and everything. Your creativity is not confined to any traditional media for making art. In fact, every choice you make is a creative one that can bring you closer to your inner artist.

Decolonize Your Mind: To examine and deconstruct the thoughts, preferences, and values that derive from a colonial way of thinking. True decolonization seeks to challenge and change white supremacy while asking us to investigate the external forces that have shaped our personal world views and identities.

Divine Purpose Path: The imaginary winding road that represents your unique journey toward living your Creative Mission. Along your path, you'll find all the breakthroughs, breakdowns, moments of bliss, hard lessons, and ecstatic experiences that have made you who you are. As you move forward, you'll begin to meet all the amazing beings you'll connect with and impact through your creative liberation. Your path won't always be clear, but if you keep taking the steps forward, it will always magically appear before you.

Elemental Archetype: This describes your unique approach to living your Creative Mission. Your elemental archetype will show you your strengths and challenges as you continue to live your Creative Mission. While you are dominant in one elemental archetype, you may also demonstrate qualities from others. The magic is in having the ability to alchemize all the elements to call upon their gifts.

Ethos: The characteristic spirit of a culture, era, or community as manifested in its beliefs and aspirations.

Flow Space: The state of mind in which you can be fully present and focused on the activities you're doing. When you are in a flow space, you are truly living in the moment. You are leading with the wisdom of your Intuitive Higher Self, without letting your anxiety or Inner Overprotectors dictate your actions or choices.

Inner Artist: The creative genius that lives inside all of us and deeply desires to be fully expressed. Every single person, without exception, has an inner artist that wants to come out and play. Your inner artist has the ability to turn your entire life into your greatest masterpiece.

Inner Overprotectors (IOPs): Another name for inner critics; those parts of yourself that might feel afraid, full of self-doubt, or deep in impostor syndrome that are actually incredibly important to your creative liberation. Their role is to protect you and help you, keeping you safe from potential harm. Once you identify your IOPs, you can begin to understand them and how they are trying to be of service to you. Then you can separate yourself from them and embrace them as quirky friends rather than trying to fight them.

Inner Muses: Intelligent beings on your spirit team that you can call upon and communicate with for creative inspiration. The more you practice communicating with your inner muses, the more you can let your relationships with them help you make divinely guided decisions that will bring you closer to your fullest expression of life.

Intention: A sacred prayer you send out to the universe. It's a path of study that guides your experience. You are constantly setting intentions, whether you realize it or not. In every moment, you are manifesting with your words, thoughts, and actions. I firmly believe that all our intentions come true.

Intuitive Higher Self: Even when you might feel confused or unsure, deeper within you, your Intuitive Higher Self knows the answers that you seek. This is the part of you that always knows your truth. The more you practice listening to your intuition, the more clearly you can hear your Intuitive Higher Self when they speak to you.

Intuitive Nudge: There is a little voice that you hear in your mind that continuously guides you toward certain actions that will bring you closer to your healing or liberation. Oftentimes, what your intuitive nudges are guiding you to do might feel scary or nerve-racking but are also equally, if not more, exhilarating. You will find more freedom on the other side of those intuitively guided steps from your spirit.

Magical Toolbox: An imaginary place where you store all of the practices, energetic or emotional tools, and healing objects that help you remember your power.

Queer: To exist outside of societal norms; to take the unconventional path in relationships and sexuality. Subversive by nature and inherently connected with the politics of liberation for all beings who fall outside of dominant identities.

Radiant Wildheart: An earth angel that is bold, fearless, and unapologetic in being truly themselves; one who is willing to take an unconventional path and an honest stand for self-expression, unafraid to be seen as they are. These healers of their lineage have limitless potential to make an impact during their time on Earth and are born to be of service. Radiant Wildhearts treat themselves with deep love and reverence, knowing that their divine offerings can change the world.

Sacred Creative Wound: The patterns and experiences that keep you from believing that you are an artist and that your work is important in the world. It prevents you from feeling truly open to self-expression and able to explore your creativity without shame or fear. Yours is unique to you, developing throughout the entirety of your life, beginning in early childhood. It's composed of all the fears, limiting beliefs, and perceived criticisms you've received and subconsciously or consciously hold on to.

Sacred Rebel: The part of you that's a trailblazer. A bridge from the old world into the new. The part of you that is unafraid to break the rules. You tap into your Sacred Rebel energy when you are not afraid to trust your intuition and lead with your values to protect the planet and the people in it. One who shuns tradition in favor of what's revolutionary and healing for the planet.

Spiral of Support: These are the people you intentionally cultivate relationships with that will support you as you live your Creative Mission. It includes your chosen community but also extends much further. People that nourish and support you as you continue to live your Creative Mission might include your trusted therapist, your accountabilibuddies, your creative collaborators, your fabulous friendships, your magical mentors, and so much more.

Spirit Team: Your spirit team consists of healed ancestors, guardian angels, plant allies, animal spirits, ascended masters, and anyone else that's been walking with you on your journey. Your spirit team's role in your life is to help you live your Creative Mission, the reason why you came onto this planet. But because you have free will, they can't help you unless you ask for it.

Stretching: Doing something that's just slightly out of your comfort zone, like setting an extra-lofty goal for yourself or being brave and doing something that scares you simply because it will help you grow and evolve. Stretching is a way of life, and I want to invite you to take the stretch when the opportunity presents itself. Nothing is going to be put in front of you that you can't handle. You're that powerful.

Shiny Object Syndrome: When you have a tendency to quickly bounce from one inspired idea to the next. Often this results in incredible projects going unfinished and taking on more than you can handle.

Spiritual Bypassing: When you hide behind spirituality in a way that prevents you from facing unresolved emotional issues or collective social issues. When you are spiritually bypassing, you might ignore the truth because it doesn't feel "high vibe" enough. However, our world holds both divinity and the shadows. Your own spiritual journey is going to be a mixed bag of positive emotions and difficult ones. Can you allow yourself to really feel it all, even those things that may not be comfortable to look at?

Endnotes

Chapter 1

1. Joanna Macy, "The Great Turning," Center for Ecoliteracy, June 29, 2009, https://www.ecoliteracy.org/article/great-turning. Macy describes the Great Turning as a shift from the Industrial Growth Society to a life-sustaining civilization.

Chapter 6

1. Trudi Lebron, *The Antiracist Business Book: An Equity Centered Approach to Work, Wealth, and Leadership* (New Egypt, NJ: Row House Publishing, 2022).

Chapter 7

1. Sandra S. Ruppert, "Critical Evidence: How the ARTS Benefit Student Achievement," National Assembly of State Arts Agencies and the Arts Education Partnership, 2006, https://files.eric.ed.gov/fulltext/ED529766.pdf.

2. Julia Cameron, *The Artist's Way: A Spiritual Path to Higher Creativity*, 25th *Anniversary Edition* (New York, NY: Penguin Random House, 2016).

Acknowledgments

It Takes a Village to Raise a Wildheart...

I deeply honor and celebrate everyone who has been a part of the journey of finding myself within these pages. I'm beyond blessed to collaborate with some of the most creatively brilliant beings in the world. From my creative spirit to yours, thank you for the support and generosity.

To my Spirit Team: To my healed ancestors, muses, and plant allies that have been divinely guiding me all along. Thank you for channeling this wisdom through me when I needed it the most. Thank you for the intuitive nudges of encouragement and truth-telling that have allowed me to reclaim the most important parts of myself and put them into service. I do it all for you.

To the elements that created everything. May this book be a love letter to you. I'm forever inspired by this planet and all its inhabitants. I want to see our Earth preserved and cherished. I want us to be around for a long time, creating art and taking it upon ourselves to beautify our community spaces. I want to see our younger generations grow up to create policy changes that are more inclusive and ethical.

When I look up at the sky, I know that I am made of stardust. I know that each one of us holds the entire universe inside of us. And our birthright is to bloom like wildflowers. The elements remind me that no matter what happens, I am always held. I can harness their wisdom to change my reality and create the world that I want to see.

To my students in the Wildheart community: Those who have trusted me, invested in my mentorship, and helped me create the healing space that I always needed. It's such a gift to be able to feel so comfortable embodying my Intuitive Highest Self while doing work that I love. Thank you for the endless inspiration and vibes. I see you and your courage, and the radical choice to express your beautiful, authentic selves in the world. Your voice is so needed and it's such an honor to walk this path with you.

To my mentors: Thank you for guiding me by holding up the magical mirror that helps me remember who I am and claim my desires. I know that I didn't get here alone, and that your Creative Mission has rippled out to impact mine in exponential ways. Thank you for your generosity in sharing your wisdom. Thank you for saying yes to your purpose and your artistry. And thank you for believing and uplifting me even in my darkest hours. In particular, I want to acknowledge Lizzy Jeff, Dr. Anjali Alimchandani, Alyssa Aparicio, and Louiza Doran for all of your support in helping me to reclaim my magic.

THIS BOOK HAS BEEN TOUCHED BY SO MANY CREATIVE HEARTS:

To Susan Ariel Rainbow Kennedy and Dr. Scott Mills: Thank you for believing in me and proving to me that my limiting belief of being too young to write a book was not true. These two devoted mentors showed me I have a book inside of me. Without both of them, I would still be an unconfident writer afraid to tell my story or go deep. The amount of energy and love they poured into me and this project does not go unnoticed. They've gone above and beyond to show me what I'm capable of and help me completely transform myself in the process. I deeply honor both SARK and Dr. Scott for their multidimensional expertise. Thank you.

To Hay House: Thank you for seeing the vision for this book before I could. I always dreamed of being published by Hay House and still can't believe that this creative dream became real. Thank for believing in me as a first-time author and giving me an inspiring and educational entry into the world of publishing. It's been so life-affirming to be asked to write a book on creativity and be encouraged at every step of the way to make this book my own. I don't take that for granted.

In particular, thank you to my fabulous editor Lisa Cheng for helping me organize my infinite thoughts and extremely long word count. I want to honor Patty Gift for seeing me and encouraging me to write an entire book about what it means to be a Radiant Wildheart. And a sincere thanks to the talented Tricia Breidenthal and the Art Department for your support in filling this book with art and helping me create something that feels truly magical. It's a huge honor to be published with Hay House.

TO THE INCREDIBLE TEAM OF ARTISTS WHO TURNED THIS BOOK INTO A WORK OF ART:

To Alexis Rakun, one of my favorite artists, for her beautiful illustrations, inspiring fairy spirit, and generosity in taking on this project. I am so grateful for her support and celebrate her Creative Mission deeply. It's an honor to collaborate with her and a creative dream come true.

To Jessie Caballero who brought our Inner Overprotectors to life. Her talent and skillset are obvious. But beyond that, her incredible connection to get her inner child is what makes her work so inspiring and special. Thank you for co-creating with me, and for all of the laughter as we bonded over our creative idiosyncrasies until we had birthed 10 loveable IOPs.

I'd also like to acknowledge **Ismaelly Peña** for her contributions to the artwork, her impeccable design aesthetic, her attention to detail, and for enriching my life in so many ways. I see your generosity and am grateful to have you on my team.

Sincere waves of gratitude for those who helped me in to conceptualize this project and sat with me through many moments of self-doubt and reinvention until I finally understood my Creative Mission. In particular, Rebekah Borucki for your mentorship and for always being willing to uplift BIPOC and LGBTQ+ voices within the publishing world. Kristen McGuinness, for helping me organize hundreds of pages of writing into a body of work that reflected the best parts of me. And Aja Vines, for helping me go deeper into some of the concepts that are fleshed out within these pages. I appreciate you all to the moon and back.

So much gratitude to my dream Radiant Wildheart team who have supported me to implement my ideas with guts and grace. In particular, I'd like to thank Christy Garcia. I'd also love to give a special shoutout to Elyse Preston and Samantha Santiago. Without you, none of this would be possible.

TO MY CHOSEN FAMILY OF FABULOUS FRIENDS, THANK YOU FOR ALL OF THE FUN TIMES THAT REMIND ME HOW HEALING IT IS TO BE IN A COMMUNITY.

Alex Valleau, Angelica Rustali, Asha Frost, Ashley Moon, Charlotte Nguyen, Kai Hernandez, Kendal White, Manny Mazaira, Nasha Mazaira, Nico Rossi, Rosa Yi, Sharrissa Iqbal, Shireen Jarrahian, Skye Noel, Sonali Fiske, Susanna Barkataki, Tara Moraleda, and Torie Feldman.

This alphabetized list is always growing. I encourage all of my readers to find their community and celebrate life with one another as often as you can.

As you can see, this book is truly a labor of love. Not just of my own, but of so many inspiring beings who were willing to come together and create something beautiful. My gratitude for each person on this list is infinite, and I wouldn't be here without you. May we continue to lift each other up and create the spaces that we always needed. May we continue to joyfully invite all Wildhearts to the table to lead from the heart and change the world.

With Love,
Shereen Sun

Radiant Wildheart

About the Author

SHEREEN SUN (she/they) is an artist, author, and acclaimed mentor on the subjects of creativity and entrepreneurship. She has spent her life living on the margins, inviting the creative spirits of others to come out and play. Shereen teaches people how to express themselves with confidence and authenticity, and she helps people live their Creative Missions by guiding them to build thriving platforms that are as impactful as they are unique.

Shereen has been an art educator since she was 18 years old. Her love for creativity and desire to help the most marginalized youth are what drove her to earn a master's in urban education with advanced specializations in the visual arts. Her love for waking up the creative spirit of others (or what she likes to call remembering their Creative Mission) led her to become an art teacher in inner city schools and paint murals with communities all around the world. After quitting her job as a teacher to start a nonprofit, she realized that she *still* wasn't living her own Creative Mission. While she loved the impact that she could have on her students, she knew that her Creative Mission was bigger than that.

Called by the desire to engage in her own creative work, she started Radiant Wildheart in 2016. It was then that she discovered that community-building actually was her creative work. By helping people to identify their passions and create a life around them, she soon found herself immersed in a community with thousands of people, with more joining every day. Her global following of loyal creatives, whom she calls Wildhearts, are longing to make a positive and creative impact on the world. She believes that everyone deserves access to the revolutionary healing power of the arts.

Shereen will always remember what it feels like to be an outsider looking for a place where she belongs. Growing up as a queer, first-generation Muslim-American in Las Vegas, she spent years feeling lost and alone. She couldn't find any career path that called to her. When she discovered the arts, she began to connect the dots and make sense of her place in the world. Now she helps others access their conscious creativity that sets them free and recognize the positive impact they have on the world.

She currently lives in Los Angeles, where you can find her teaching at music festivals, working on her latest song, painting with friends, and loving life. Learn more about her by visiting www.radiantwildheart.com.

Hay House Titles of Related Interest

YOU CAN HEAL YOUR LIFE, the movie, starring Louise Hay & Friends
(available as an online streaming video)
www.hayhouse.com/louise-movie

THE SHIFT, the movie,
starring Dr. Wayne W. Dyer
(available as an online streaming video)
www.hayhouse.com/the-shift-movie

✦ ✦ ✦

A YEAR OF MYSTICAL THINKING: Make Life Feel Magical Again, by Emma Howarth

*LETTERS TO A STARSEED: Messages and Activations for Remembering
Who You Are and Why You Came Here,* by Rebecca Campbell

*OWN YOUR GLOW: A Soulful Guide to Luminous Living and
Crowning the Queen Within,* by Latham Thomas

RADICAL SELF-LOVE: A Guide to Loving Yourself and Living Your Dreams,
by Gala Darling

*YOU ARE MORE THAN YOU THINK YOU ARE: Practical Enlightenment
for Everyday Life,* by Kimberly Snyder

All of the above are available at your local bookstore,
or may be ordered by contacting Hay House (see next page).

✦ ✦ ✦

We hope you enjoyed this Hay House book. If you'd like to receive our online catalog featuring additional information on Hay House books and products, or if you'd like to find out more about the Hay Foundation, please contact:

Hay House, Inc., P.O. Box 5100, Carlsbad, CA 92018-5100
(760) 431-7695 or (800) 654-5126
(760) 431-6948 (fax) or (800) 650-5115 (fax)
www.hayhouse.com® • www.hayfoundation.org

———

Published in Australia by: Hay House Australia Pty. Ltd.,
18/36 Ralph St., Alexandria NSW 2015
Phone: 612-9669-4299 • *Fax:* 612-9669-4144
www.hayhouse.com.au

Published in the United Kingdom by: Hay House UK, Ltd.,
The Sixth Floor, Watson House, 54 Baker Street, London W1U 7BU
Phone: +44 (0)20 3927 7290 • *Fax:* +44 (0)20 3927 7291
www.hayhouse.co.uk

Published in India by: Hay House Publishers India,
Muskaan Complex, Plot No. 3, B-2, Vasant Kunj, New Delhi 110 070
Phone: 91-11-4176-1620 • *Fax:* 91-11-4176-1630
www.hayhouse.co.in

———

Access New Knowledge.
Anytime. Anywhere.

Learn and evolve at your own pace
with the world's leading experts.

www.hayhouseU.com